ZAMBIA
SAFARI IN STYLE

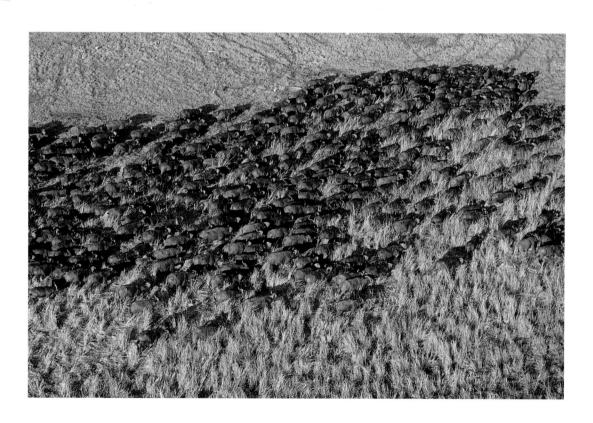

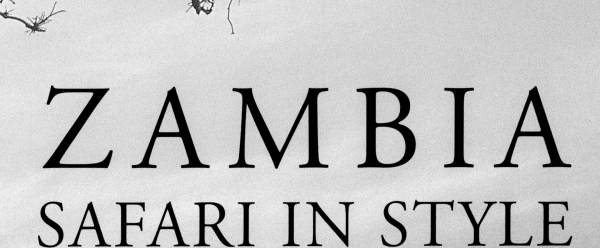

ZAMBIA
SAFARI IN STYLE

intimate travel experiences exploring the
wilds & wonders of Zambia

DAVID ROGERS

AFRICA
Geographic

When **British Airways'** forerunner, Imperial Airways, pioneered an airline service between the United Kingdom and southern Africa, its weekly passenger flights stopped over in the Zambian town of Mpika to refuel and embark and disembark passengers.

This marked the beginning of an association with Zambia that has developed and strengthened over some 70 years.

Today Africa's potential as a hub for nature-based and cultural tourism is immense and British Airways recognises the economic significance of this for the people of Africa.

We are proud, therefore, to be associated with the publication of *Zambia – Safari in Style.*

This beautiful book explores the wide-ranging nature-based travel opportunities to be found within the borders of this remarkably diverse country. Its purpose in showcasing Zambia's wildlife, lodges, game reserves and national parks reflects British Airways' commitment to helping ensure that the country is recognised as one of Africa's prime destinations.

Charles Forsyth
British Airways General Manager East &
Southern Africa and Indian Ocean Islands

BRITISH AIRWAYS

contents

Introducing Zambia 8

Above the Falls 10
Mutemwa Lodge 12
Stanley Safari Lodge 18
Sussi Lodge & Chuma House 24
The River Club 32
Thorntree River Lodge 38
Tongabezi Lodge 42

Below the Falls 46
Chiawa Camp 48
Old Mondoro 52
Sausage Tree Camp 54
Kulefu Tented Camp 60

Valley of Leopards 64
Buffalo Camp 66
Chichele Presidential Lodge &
    Puku Ridge Tented Camp 68
Kafunta River Lodge & Island
    Bush Camp 76
Mfuwe Lodge & The Bushcamp
    Company 82
Norman Carr Safaris 88
Remote Africa Safaris 94
Robin Pope Safaris 100
Shenton Safaris 108

Highlands of Plenty 114
Chaminuka Lodge 116
Lechwe Plains Tented Camp 122
Lunga River Lodge & Busanga
    Bushcamp 126

Into the North 132
Kapishya 134
Shiwa Ng'andu 136
Kasanka 138

Travel Advisory 142

introducing
zambia

Over the past decade I have been fortunate to visit Zambia many times. I have waded through the Bangweulu Swamps in search of shoebills, watched elephants crossing the Lower Zambezi, seen fabulous flowers blooming on the Liuwa Plains and observed countless leopards in the Luangwa. Every moment has been memorable. The country has an incredible draw for me – the more I see, the more I want to see. And the people, who are warm, friendly and thoroughly welcoming, make it extra special.

Ten per cent of Zambia is protected by national parks and game reserves, and these areas showcase the country's extraordinary biodiversity.

South Luangwa, which is one of the best places to see predators such as leopard, is Zambia's flagship national park, with outstanding lodges. At Mosi oa Tunya National Park the fabulous Victoria Falls thunders its worth as one of the great natural wonders of the world. Further along is the Lower Zambezi National Park where elephants, hippos and lions provide an even wilder experience for nature lovers. Then there are North Luangwa, Kasanka, Lochinvar, Liuwa Plains and Sioma Ngwezi, all of which offer their own special attractions from mammals and birds to bats, flowers and wetlands.

After Zambian independence in 1964, and until about 15 years ago, commercial poachers shot hundreds of thousands of wild animals, including elephant, buffalo and the entire rhino population. The poaching situation has since improved tremendously, and the fact that there are any animals left in Zambia is largely due to private tourism operators and the Zambian Wildlife Authority, whose combined presence has helped to keep poachers at bay.

Tourism in Zambia is of substantial benefit to its wildlife, and to its people, who suffer greatly from underemployment, inadequate education and the massive incidence of HIV/Aids.

Visit any of the lodges that appear in this book and not only are you assured of a great tourism experience, but you will also be helping to put this beautiful country back on track.

A village scene near the entrance to Lochinvar National Park.

Beer is sold by the ladle at Maramba Market in Livingstone.

Village children wave at a passing boat on the Kafue Flats.

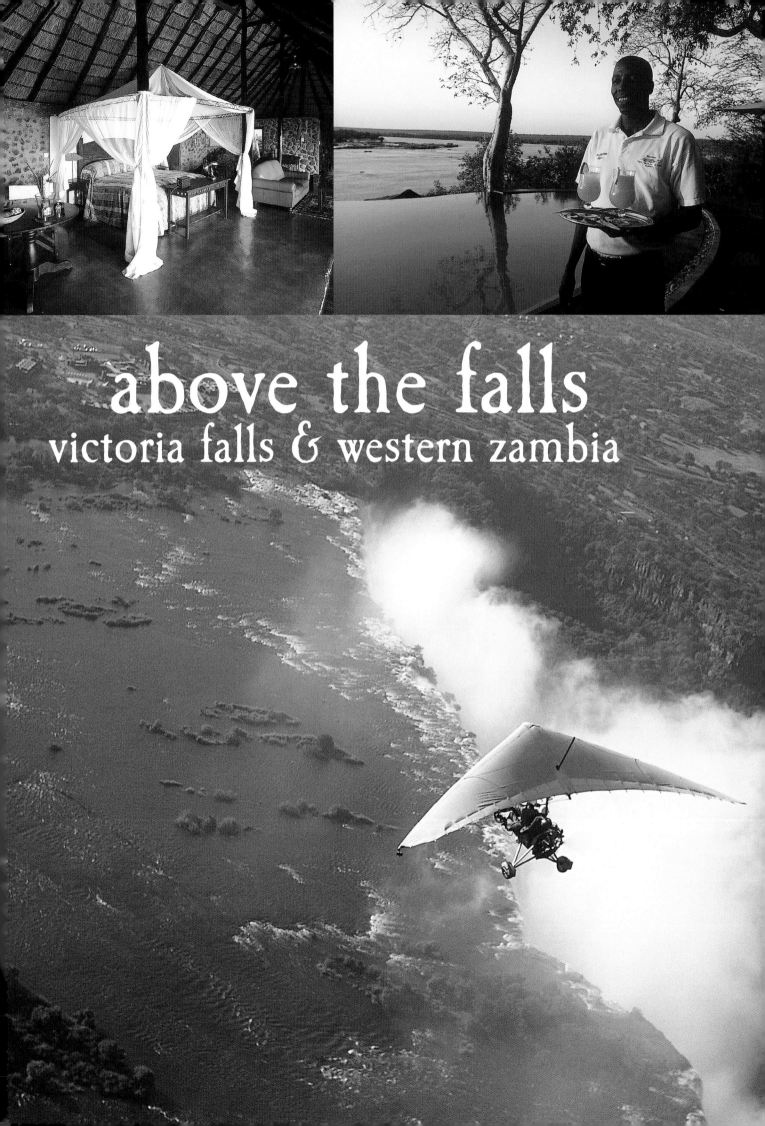

above the falls
victoria falls & western zambia

The mighty Zambezi River draws
its waters from the swampy
reaches of western Zambia,
gathering momentum before its
finest moment at Victoria Falls.
Here, the two-kilometre wide
river plunges over the escarpment
and gives off the thunderous roar
that has earned it the name,
'the smoke that thunders'.

Microlighting above Victoria Falls.

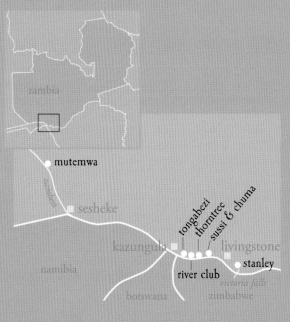

mutemwa lodge
western zambia

Owned by former Springbok rugby player, Gavin Johnson, Mutemwa fishing and birding lodge offers a homely base from which to explore exciting western Zambia.

like many great fishing and birding camps, the emphasis is more on what happens outside the tent flaps

Mutemwa Lodge is remote in its location about 250 kilometres upstream from Victoria Falls on the fringe of western Zambia's Barotse Plains. It is owned by former Springbok rugby player Gavin Johnson, who was part of South Africa's winning squad in the 1995 World Cup. Since then, he has put all his rugby earnings into the game-driving vehicles, fishing boats, canvas and planks that have transformed Mutemwa into the most established lodge in western Zambia.

In the bar is the jersey he wore at the World Cup and several photographs of match-winning moments, but these days the lanky fullback seems much more interested in panning the skies with his Swarovski binoculars than with following the high ball. He is now a dedicated family man, who told me he doesn't like going anywhere without Penny and his two young daughters.

I have always remembered Gavin as the neatest player to run onto the field – and his lodge is equally well presented. The six comfortable tents all have en-suite bathrooms, the lawns are neatly trimmed and the swimming pool, boats and vehicles are spotless. Like many great fishing and birding camps, the emphasis at Mutemwa is more on what happens outside the tent flaps than on the décor.

Penny is a charming hostess, who also keeps the books and runs the kitchens at the lodge. She is down-to-earth and friendly, and prides herself on serving good, wholesome, homemade food – and lots of it!

Others in the Mutemwa family include Devan van der Merwe who, despite being only a few years out of school, is already a Springbok fisherman. 'I feel like I'm in heaven,' he enthused. 'There are places here that have hardly ever been fished – and we can go there anytime for great bream and tigers.'

Mutemwa's specialist birding guide, Cuan Rush, was an apprentice to Guy Gibbon, and

PREVIOUS SPREAD Springbok fisherman and Mutemwa guide, Devan van der Merwe tests his skill at catching tigerfish in a Zambezi rapid.

Mutemwa's tents are airy and comfortable.

One of the tents, as seen from the river.

THIS SPREAD Gavin is a family man who doesn't go anywhere without Penny and his daughters, Shan and Cayla.

Breakfasts and lunches are served on a deck beside the river. While sitting there, we were able to tick off 'camp regulars' such as Schalow's turaco.

From the deck of each tent there is a magnificent view of the Zambezi.

Swimming at Sioma Falls, a natural jacuzzi.

with 450 of Zambia's recorded 740 species found in this region, the great birding never seems to stop. Out on the wide Zambezi River we watched hundreds of yellow-billed kites spiralling above the forest canopy as they feasted on a bounty of hatching termites. We also saw African skimmers raking the shallow waters with their long red beaks, African finfoot and, within the camp, a host of birds including African paradise-flycatchers and Schalow's turacos.

The lodge is about three hours' drive from the stunningly beautiful Ngonye Falls, which were first documented by David Livingstone in 1854, two years before he reached Victoria Falls.

'…the river is confined in a space of not more than one hundred yards wide. The water goes boiling along, and gives the idea of great masses of it rolling over and over… Viewed from the mass of rock which overhangs the falls, the scenery was the loveliest I had seen.'

Even today the falls are remote and seldom visited. As I paddled across to the vantage point by canoe, I too felt thrilled by the adventure of it all.

My travels with Gavin took me about 400 kilometres north of Mutemwa to the Liuwa Plains, which is something of a holy grail for wildlife enthusiasts due to its remoteness and phenomenal fauna and flora. We saw wonderful flocks of crowned and wattled cranes and a notable abundance of raptors.

Gavin set up a tented camp at Royal Pools, a site that is traditionally used by the Lozi king, and from here we went on forays through the park. It was soon after the first rains and some 15 000 wildebeest had followed the billowing clouds onto the lush plains in a phenomenal congregation reminiscent of the Serengeti migration. The plains were bejewelled with spectacular brunsvigias and

a host of animals, including oribi, tsessebe, zebra, red lechwe, reedbuck and dozens of hyaenas.

After the summer rains, when the Barotse Plain becomes flooded, Gavin takes tourists to see the annual Kuomboka Ceremony and to join thousands of Lozi people who turn out to watch their king being transported on rising floodwaters from his summer palace to his winter palace in a massive wooden canoe that is paddled by about 150 men.

The Lozi king has an interest in the conservation of his region and its wildlife and is also a partner in Gavin's determined drive to increase the thrust of tourism into the wild and wonderfully wet western Zambia.

The Sioma Ngwezi National Park, which is about two hours' drive from the lodge, also begs to be explored. It borders on the Kwando River and has a fantastic diversity of species, including roan and sable antelope, tsessebe, Livingstone's eland, buffalo, giraffe and elephant, as well as lion, leopard, cheetah and wild dog.

Gavin and Penny's dream is to have an influence on Sioma Ngwezi so that it will thrive with wildlife again and to uplift the Lozi people through tourism. Only in this way, they say, will this beautiful piece of Africa be conserved for generations to come.

Sundowners on the Liuwa Plains.

A lone wildebeest surrounded by brunsvigias on the Liuwa Plains.

Guests usually eat dinner around the fire, or on a balcony overlooking the river.

my travels with Gavin took me to the Liuwa Plains, which is something of a holy grail for wildlife enthusiasts

details

When to go
The best time for birding is during the wet months, from November to April. The fish are biting from March through to November. Liuwa Plains is at its best in November and December.

How to get there
Mutemwa is a three-hour drive (the last 50 kilometres are on rutted dirt) or a half-hour flight from Livingstone. Liuwa is a two-day drive across the Barotse floodplain or a two-hour flight from Livingstone.

Who to contact
Tel. (+27-11) 234 1747, (+27-82) 990 2405, e-mail *mutemwa.lodge@mweb.co.za* or go to *www.mutemwa.com*

Built into the hills overlooking

Victoria Falls, the Stanley is a

stylish lodge from which to

explore this exciting region.

safari lodge

victoria falls area

1 **Having searched the banks** of the Zambezi for the perfect location for a lodge, Vinciane and Reinout de Gruijter knew they had found it when they climbed an ancient msasa tree and saw infinite views along the length of the Zambezi, across the falls and to the hills of Zimbabwe. At this site they built an exquisite lodge from the wood and stone that is found naturally in the area.

Vinciane, the architect of the pair, says, 'The inspiration for the Stanley comes from the paradise that it bestrides. All that I have done is echo the natural wonder. The fire of the setting sun and the smooth waters of the Zambezi are mirrored across space in the lodge. So from the water of our infinity pool to the fire of the great hearth of the main house we have reflected our view: fire – water – air – water – fire. It's so simple!'

PREVIOUS SPREAD The honeymoon suite.

Victoria Falls, viewed from Livingstone Island.

The de Gruijters have made imaginative use of local materials, as seen in this light-shade.

THIS SPREAD Views of the bushveld seem endless from the fringe of the lodge.

The lodge is owned by an architect, who has implemented elegant lines and an intimate layout that works.

You'll have to travel far to find more romantic bathrooms than those in the African suites.

Each suite has its own private plunge pool.

Wood carvings at the nearby Mukuni Village.

STANLEY SAFARI LODGE

they saw
infinite views
along the
length of the
Zambezi

most of the chalets
are built of stone
and thatch and are
completely open to
the west and to the
cooling breezes that
blow in from the hills

Elephant-back safaris are just one of the activities that can be arranged from Stanley Safari Lodge.

The spacious Family Room.

A romantic breakfast, served in the pool that's within sight of the spray from Victoria Falls.

With three staff members allocated to each guest, you are well looked after.

Recently rated eleven out of ten on the 'Romantic Richter Scale', the Stanley was also described by *Good Taste* magazine in 2004 as 'one of the most stylish boutique hotels in the world'.

Most of the 10 chalets are built of stone and thatch and are completely open to the west and to the cooling breezes that blow in from the hills. These open sides allow you to see the most incredible sunsets from anywhere in your room – the bed, the bath and in some cases even the loo! The African and colonial suites have their own private plunge pools and the most romantic baths I have ever seen.

While the stone-and-thatch chalets are decorated with African artwork and have an ethnic feel, the colonial suites reflect the elegance of Livingstone and Stanley's era, with heavy wooden doors, high ceilings, elegant four-poster beds and en-suite lounges.

Dining at the Stanley is exceptional. The menu changes daily, but rather than choose what to eat, you can choose *where* to eat. The main house has been designed to incorporate space, views and intimacy, and offers a choice of dining areas both inside and out. You can dine privately in your chalet or celebrate a special occasion with a quiet meal beside the pool. Breakfasts can be served on the deck, in the library, the wine cellar or the pool, or anywhere else you fancy.

The Stanley is an ideal base from which to experience the wonders of the Vic Falls area, yet it is secluded from the bustle and high-powered activity of Livingstone.

The Victoria Falls and the Zambezi need little introduction and the Stanley's courteous, friendly and knowledgeable staff can guide you to the pleasures that they offer. From canoeing and elephant-back safaris to swimming at the lip of the falls, microlighting and white-water rafting if you're feeling adventurous, there's quite a choice.

STANLEY SAFARI LODGE

STANLEY SAFARI LODGE

STANLEY SAFARI LODGE

details

When to go
Vic Falls is most spectacular after the rains in March and April. September and October are the best months for white-water rafting and game viewing.

How to get there
Stanley Safari Lodge is a half-hour drive from Livingstone International Airport.

Who to contact
Stanley Safari Lodge. Tel. (+260-97) 84 8615, (+263-91) 26 2042, e-mail *info@stanleysafaris.com* or go to *www.stanleysafaris.com*

sussi lodge &

chuma house

mosi oa tunya national park

Named after Livingstone's two bearers,

Star of Africa's exclusive lodges are situated on

the bank of the Zambezi River.

The names given to Sussi Lodge and Chuma House pay tribute to the two faithful Zambian bearers who bravely carried David Livingstone's body for 1 500 kilometres from the fringe of the Bangweulu Swamps, where he died in 1873, to the port of Dar es Salaam, where it was shipped to London and interned at Westminster Abbey.

The lodge was completed in 2002 by Star of Africa as the flagship for its spectacular Zambian circuit, which also includes two properties in South Luangwa and others in Lower Zambezi and Lochinvar national parks. Co-owner Dave Bennett was also the architect of the Amalinda Lodge in Zimbabwe, which became famous for its innovative style (it is built into rocks) and outstanding service. Dave runs Star of Africa with John Glendinning, a well-known entrepreneur who specialises in building and construction and has been responsible for the construction and logistical support for the lodges.

Sussi and Chuma are two separate properties and, despite their close proximity, are entirely self-contained and privately situated along the bank of the Zambezi River, about 10 kilometres upstream from Victoria Falls. Sharing a setting in a natural inlet within the Mosi oa Tunya National Park, they overlook a series of rapids and islands frequented by vervet monkeys and elephants.

Sussi Lodge is the larger of the two properties and comprises a string of 10 exquisite lodges that have been built under a canopy of ebony trees. The suites each have a large bedroom with walk-in mosquito net,

PREVIOUS SPREAD The lounge at Chuma House has homely comforts as well as satellite television and Internet access.

Sussi style – a sandy island, the setting sun, and drinks in the cooler.

A delicately carved wooden bench in the gardens at Chuma House.

THIS SPREAD The white rhinos that were re-introduced to the zoological park are under constant guard from poachers.

Sussi's double-storey lodge has 10 chalets connected by boardwalks.

All the rooms have overhead fans and walk-in mosquito nets.

Chuma is an exclusive house with two double bedrooms and its own team of staff.

Sussi and Chuma pay tribute to the two
faithful Zambian bearers who bravely carried
David Livingstone's body for 1 500 kilometres

bar fridge, overhead fan and a spectacular bathroom and deck overlooking the river. They are connected to the main reception area by a series of boardwalks, which are several metres above the ground. This makes getting about easier – especially at night when hippos and elephants move through the unfenced property on their way to and from the river. Even from the safety of the boardwalk, it's a heart-stopping experience walking over creaking planks with hippos and elephants grazing below.

Sussi's dining and pool area, which overlooks the Zambezi, is a dramatic double-storey construction that is great for relaxing with a cold drink and dining under the stars on balmy nights. It's made entirely from natural materials with a thatched roof, wooden decks and a pool that mirrors the colour of the river. Like the rest of the lodge, its décor is a charming mix of African colours, curios and artistry. Black and white pictures of Sussi and Chuma grace the walls, along with carved artworks and African

prints, while small Bushmen figurines guard the winding staircases that lead up from the swimming deck to the lounge and bar.

Chuma is a self-contained house with two double bedrooms, a central lounge area (with satellite television and modem points), a kitchen, a swimming pool and a private barbecue area. It's so close to the water that you can stand on the lawn and cast for tiger and bream.

Both lodges have their own staff and similar activities, including game-viewing cruises on the river and trips to Victoria Falls and Mosi oa Tunya Zoological Park.

My guide, Samuel Simunji, was the son of one of the previous rangers in the park and as we purred around in the most exclusive open-topped luxury game-drive vehicle I have ever encountered, he provided me with fascinating insights into the natural and human history of the region. Much of the park falls within an area previously called Old Drift where the first white settlers made their homes in the 19th century.

Sussi has been built from natural materials and blends beautifully into the forest.

Chuma House has all the conveniences of a home, including a kitchen and its own private swimming pool.

Sussi's elegant staircase winds in great sweeps from the pool to the dining room.

Dung beetles busy themselves with fresh elephant droppings on the forest floor.

it's so close to the water that you can stand on the lawn and cast for tiger and bream

It extends for about 10 kilometres along the Zambezi and provides refuge for impala, buffalo, zebra, giraffe and bushbuck, as well as a pair of white rhinos that were introduced from South Africa. Being among the few rhinos in Zambia, they have 24-hour guards who safeguard them from poachers. On the whole, it's a fairly tame reserve, but the game is relaxed and it's particularly scenic at sunrise when the forest and the river catch the first rays of light.

Sussi and Chuma are already outstanding destinations, but Star of Africa has more plans. They intend to build two more self-contained houses at Chuma.

The pool at Sussi was designed to mirror the colour of the Zambezi.

During the dry season, elephants converge on the banks of the Zambezi in search of food and water.

The view of the Zambezi from the main lodge is of a series of rapids and islands that can be explored.

it's particularly scenic at sunrise when the forest and the river catch the first rays of light

details

When to go
Sussi and Chuma are open throughout the year. Victoria Falls is fullest during April and May, but is also spectacular when the water is low and more of the falls are visible through the mist. October is the best time for white-water rafting.

How to get there
Sussi and Chuma are 25 minutes' drive from Livingstone International Airport.

Who to contact
Star of Africa. Tel. (+260-1) 27 1508/9, e-mail *reservations@starofafrica.co.zm* or go to *www.star-of-africa.com*

the river club

above the falls

The colonial River Club offers a royal welcome

upstream of Victoria Falls on the Zambezi.

PREVIOUS SPREAD Wide views of the Zambezi and its sandy islands are the focus of the River Club – even from the swimming pool.

THIS SPREAD Canoeing on the Lower Zambezi.

Downstairs, and right on the water's edge, are the bathrooms.

Novias Mulife has been serving drinks and welcoming guests at the River Club since it started seven years ago.

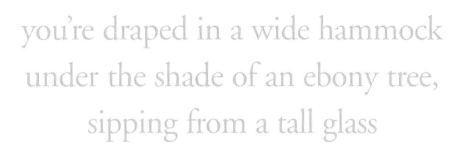

you're draped in a wide hammock
under the shade of an ebony tree,
sipping from a tall glass

Picture the scene. You're draped in a wide hammock under the shade of an ebony tree, sipping from a tall glass and staring out over the wind-rippled surface of the Zambezi. Hippos lie lazily in the shallows and elephants paddle and blow on the far river-bank. It is quiet, apart from the tinkle of ice in your glass, the slow tick of the sprinkler and robins calling sweetly from the trees.

This is the River Club, an exclusive Edwardian-style lodge on the forested northern bank of the Zambezi, about 20 kilometres upstream from Victoria Falls.

Master of the club is the charismatic Peter Jones, an ex-British Army officer and former Zambezi rafting guide, who prides himself on maintaining the dignified habits of the British Empire – even in wild, dusty Africa.

At dinner, for example, Peter carefully seated all the guests himself in order to make sure the balance was right. We were then served by waiters impeccably dressed in white uniforms, maroon skullcaps and sashes. And what occasion would have been proper without port? Once its lid had been crushed, the bottle began its anti-clockwise orbit of the large teak table. Everyone was requested to take part and those who declined were politely encouraged to make amends by blowing an old brass bugle. We rounded off the hilarious evening with a game of croquet. Lanterns had been lit beside each hoop, drinks were served at a small table and, to keep the bugs at bay, waiters stood ready with tins of insect repellent on silver trays.

The River Club has 10 sumptuous rooms that are named after explorers and colonial figures like Livingstone, Stanley and Selous. Each room is on two levels, with bedrooms upstairs and bathrooms below. The bathrooms are a real highlight, being so close to the river that you can almost touch the water. On the walls are pictures of hunters and explorers, and Punch cartoons make light-hearted fun of the eccentric British character.

The River Club also offers a wonderful library filled with tales of African adventurers, and massages can be enjoyed in a glorious calico tent overlooking the river. You can take your own trip to the falls, where microlight flights, helicopter trips and museum tours are among the highlights. Or you can simply relax next to the River Club's swimming pool and contemplate the glorious views, like I did.

The River Club has made a substantial effort to help the nearby Simonga village by ensuring that a ready supply of drinking water reaches the community of about 3 000 people. It has also been instrumental in the education of the community's children by assisting with the construction of a school building and in supplying the children with books and stationery.

Tranquil sunset cruises on the Zambezi give guests a chance to enjoy the dramatic scenery and catch sight of elephants coming to drink.

If the river doesn't soothe your troubles, you can opt for massage therapy!

The suites take their names from African explorers and have views of the river.

on the walls were pictures of hunters and explorers,
and Punch cartoons which make light-hearted fun of
the eccentric British character

details

Getting there
The River Club is a half-hour drive
from Livingstone International Airport,
with an additional 10-minute boat
transfer to camp.

When to go
The River Club is open throughout
the year, and every month has its own
attraction. Vic Falls is most spectacular
after the rains in March and April.

Who to contact
Wilderness Safaris. Tel. (+27-11)
807 1800, e-mail
enquiries@wilderness.co.za or go to
www.wilderness-safaris.com

thorntree river lodge

mosi oa tunya national park

Zambia's adrenalin-sport specialist,

Safari Par Excellence, also owns

a lodge that is guaranteed to have a

much more relaxing effect.

Safari Par Excellence has been an adventure specialist at Livingstone and Victoria Falls for 15 years and has developed an outstanding safety record in what is widely regarded as the most exciting commercial one-day rafting trip in the world. It's a mind-bogglingly thrilling day on the Zambezi River, with rapids that left me wide-eyed, wet and wanting more.

'SafPar' has also become involved in more leisurely pursuits and recently opened a luxury establishment called Thorntree River Lodge about 12 kilometres upstream of the falls. Far away from the buzz of town and inside the Mosi oa Tunya National Park, Thorntree is a most relaxing and unpretentious place to kick back and relax, and enjoy good food and comfortable accommodation right on the edge of the river. There are boat trips, game drives and fishing trips on offer in addition to the long list of activities at the falls.

Adventure never seems to be far away from SafPar. One evening, after a delightful dinner of chickens cooked in beer on an open fire, followed by delectable tiramisu and all served under the stars, three full-grown hippos joined the party and blocked the paths back to our rooms. 'I'm afraid it's road transfers this evening,' manager Nick Lynch offered amiably, and then drove us through the gauntlet back to our rooms.

Other frequent guests at the lodge are a group of six African elephants that belong to sister company Zambezi Elephant Trails, which is run by Clover King, a young Canadian woman with deep blue, gentle eyes that seem just the thing to melt the hearts of even the most obstreperous elephant bulls.

'The animals were previously orphaned and have been brought together from different parks in Zimbabwe to make one happy family,' she told me. 'During the day they roam free, and at night they congregate in a purpose-built enclosure, which ensures constant physical contact between them. They are trained by positive reinforcement, with no fear of pain, and all encouragement is followed by reward.'

The elephant trails last over an hour and have no set route. Although a guide leads the elephants through the bush at his own discretion, the elephants' personalities emerge as they show their preferences to lead, follow, walk through water or avoid it. When our entourage finally returned to camp, Clover invited us to interact with the elephants and to reward them with pellets. 'Feel here,' she said, pressing my hand against the thick hide of Mushumbi's swollen belly. 'She eloped in January 2003 with some wild elephant bulls,' she said. 'When she came back 10 months later, the wayward child was healthy – and pregnant.'

other frequent guests at the lodge are a group of six African elephants

PREVIOUS SPREAD Thorntree River Lodge is visited by six tame African elephants that take guests on trails through the park.

THIS SPREAD Because hippos mow the lawns outside the lodges, guests need to take care when walking to and from the dining room.

Some 50 000 adventure seekers go white-water rafting on the Zambezi every year.

Stone walls and high thatched roofs make the rooms cool and comfortable, even in summer.

Quick, give him a treat – or he might join you in the pool.

Early risers are rewarded with good bird sightings from the deck.

details

When to go
Thorntree River Lodge is open throughout the year. Vic Falls is most spectacular after the rains in March and April. White-water rafting is best when the water level is low in September and October.

How to get there
Thorntree Lodge is a 10-kilometre drive from Livingstone International Airport.

Who to contact
Safari Par Excellence. Tel. (+263) 444 3409/10, e-mail *speres@mweb.co.zw* or go to *www.safpar.com*

tongabezi lodge
victoria falls area

Livingstone's original luxury
lodge has a proud reputation
based on romance, grand
adventure and integrity.

When Englishmen Ben Parker and the late Will Ruck-Keene started Tongabezi Lodge in 1990, the intimate, exquisite and original lodge soon became talked about in the highest of circles. It earned its place as one of the most romantic destinations on earth and the *New York Times* even wrote that the Honeymoon Suite was worth getting married for.

Over the years I have spent glorious times at Tongabezi, sleeping with the Zambezi close to my feet in riverside rooms such as the Bird House, the Dog House and the Honeymoon Suite, and calling for my tea or coffee using the antiquated wind-up telephones that are one of the curious features of the lodge. I've enjoyed birding on islands in the river with the lodge's friendly staff and sipping local beers from vendors at the colourful Maramba market in Livingstone.

Tongabezi has a wonderful history and Ben Parker, who lives there, has an adventurous spirit akin to David Livingstone's. Over the years, he has lured me on all sorts of journeys throughout Zambia by microlight and canoe.

One of the most exciting expeditions Ben offers is the trip to Livingstone Island, which is the spot where the great explorer first viewed the falls. Here we drank tea, ate lunch, and took a heart-stopping swim by jumping into a rock pool in the middle of the Zambezi, right beside a 100-metre drop. This must rate as one of my most thrilling experiences ever. But that is not the end of it. 'Look below,' Ben advised,

handing me a mask. Much to my amazement, we weren't alone in the pool. Diving beneath the surface, I goggled at a school of small fish swimming right against the lip of the massive drop.

Tongabezi is, and always has been, mostly about romance. Meals for two can be served on a floating barge in the middle of the Zambezi. For those who want an even quieter experience, there's Sindabezi Island with its own private staff, gas lighting and absolute solitude. For the most exclusive Tongabezi experience, groups of up to eight people can book into Tangala House, an exquisitely designed home on the banks of the Zambezi River.

Zambian people are known to be extremely friendly, and this is apparent among the staff of Tongabezi. The lodge has always employed and trained local staff and encouraged them to meet and speak with guests. Much of the credit for the lodge's good spirit must go to Ben's wife, Vanessa, who has given her time to the Tujatane School, which she started in the grounds of the lodge. Tujatane means 'let's all hold hands together' and the school supports 116 children, including those of the lodge staff, who receive first-rate education from four qualified teachers. Tujatane is equipped with television, computers and a library of books, all of which have been donated by visitors to the lodge. In its most recent newsletter, the school was delighted to report it had taken first place in a national poetry competition. Now that is something.

PREVIOUS SPREAD Summer explorations of the falls require wet-weather gear.

What better way to spend a honeymoon than canoeing up the Zambezi?

The *sanpan* dinners at Tongabezi are served on a barge in the river, with waiters arriving by boat.

THIS SPREAD Lodge owner Ben Parker shows his adventurous style in this precarious leap into a cliff-side pool on Livingstone Island.

Tongabezi's bedrooms set a standard for romantic accommodation, with beautiful views of the river.

The highly acclaimed Tujatane School is sponsored by guests of the lodge and run by Vanessa Parker.

Butler service is just a quick call away on the quirky wind-up telephones.

The Zambezi flows within metres of Tongabezi's deck and dining area.

we took a
heart-stopping
swim by jumping
into a rock pool
in the middle of
the Zambezi

details

When to go
Vic Falls is most spectacular after the
rains in March and April. October is the
best time for white-water rafting and
game viewing, and swimming on
Livingstone Island.

How to get there
From Livingstone International Airport
it's a half-hour drive to Tongabezi.

Who to contact
Tongabezi Lodge. Tel. (+260-3)
32 4450 or 32 4468, e-mail
reservations@tongabezi.com
or go to *www.tongabezi.com*

below the falls

lower zambezi national park

Lower Zambezi National Park lies opposite Mana Pools in Zimbabwe and shares with it a similar habitat of winterthorn-tree forest that fringes the mighty Zambezi River and attracts large herds of elephants. Outstanding game reserves in this region offer a wonderful combination of game drives, boat trips and some of the best tigerfishing in the world.

Drifting past elephants in the Lower Zambezi National Park.

Chiawa was the first camp to

open in the Lower Zambezi,

and it has played a major role in

the park's conservation. It has

also developed a reputation as

a superbly run operation,

with excellent guiding and

outstanding cuisine.

chiawa camp
lower zambezi national park

'We were the only operators in the park when we got here in 1989,' said Grant Cumings, owner of Chiawa Camp. 'At that time the Lower Zambezi was as much a green patch on the map as a national park, with rampant poaching and little control.' In 1995 Grant was one of the founding members of Conservation Lower Zambezi, a privately funded organisation that provides logistical support, education and training to the dedicated but under-funded Zambian Wildlife Authority and has done much to stop poaching. The game has settled down well and out of 200 game-viewing days recorded in one year, Grant's team notched up 249 separate sightings of lion and 175 of leopard.

With its extensive view over the Zambezi River towards Mana Pools National Park, Chiawa's location is spectacular. It has become one of Zambia's most popular camps, and guests return year after year to enjoy the Cumings' legendary hospitality and exemplary level of organisation.

I visited Chiawa in early October when it was hot and steamy, and elephants and buffalos crowded the riverbanks as they alternated between wallowing in the cool water during the heat of the day and feasting on the winterthorn pods that lay strewn on the ground.

Game viewing is also good from the platforms situated above the *chitenge* and where the Chowe River spills into the Zambezi. But you can even watch game from your private tent, though you should be cautious in getting to and from it!

One evening, a relaxing boat trip along the river turned into a night drive as we drove back to camp to the sound of lions roaring loudly. There is a dominant pair in this region and we tracked them down to a clearing, where we watched them rolling around together in the dust. Finally, the promise of delectable cuisine drew us back to camp.

Then, while the frogs sent their greetings into the night, we considered our options for the following day: watching elephant by canoe sounded like a grand idea, but then so did fishing in the Zambezi. Chiawa's record for tigerfish is a whopping 10 kilograms, and that seemed like a fine score to beat.

*you can even
watch game
from your
private tent*

PREVIOUS SPREAD The characteristic four-winged shape of a combretum's seed pod.

Chiawa Camp, as seen from the Zambezi River, with the escarpment as its spectacular backdrop.

A saddle-billed stork waits patiently in one of the small tributaries flowing off the escarpment.

THIS SPREAD A spectacular Chiawa dinner, served in a dry riverbed.

Elephants frequently cross the Zambezi in front of the camp.

Chiawa's 'Superior Safari Tent', with its spectacular bathroom.

Another tigerfish caught at Chiawa, but soon to be returned to the river.

The excellent guides at Chiawa are always on the lookout for interesting sights – in this case a large caterpillar web.

details

When to go
Chiawa is open from mid-April to mid-November. The best months for fishing are September to November, and game viewing (by vehicle, foot, canoe and motorboat) is best between July and November, although May and June can be excellent too.

How to get there
There are daily 40-minute charters from Lusaka to the Lower Zambezi's Royal and Jeki airstrips. Chiawa will collect you from either airstrip, with each transfer taking about an hour.

Who to contact
Chiawa Camp. Tel. (+260-1) 26 1588, e-mail *info@chiawa.com* or go to *www.chiawa.com*

old mondoro
lower zambezi national park

Old Mondoro

provides guests with a

remote and authentic

safari that focuses on

wildlife and the bush

experience.

Old Mondoro is the smallest and most intimate of the lodges in the Lower Zambezi National Park. It's a simple bush camp situated deep inside the park, with an open-sided *chitenge* and four reed-and-thatch chalets that crouch on the river's edge beneath a forest of ancient and gnarled acacia trees.

From the camp, elephants can often be seen crossing the river while hippos lie in the shallows and crocodiles bask on the banks. Paraffin lamps provide light, and water for showering is heated over the fire. The effect is quite magical, and I had a sense that humankind had touched this part of the earth very lightly.

Old Mondoro is a joint venture between Chiawa Camp and Sausage Tree Camp, and is offered exclusively, almost as an 'added extra', to guests staying at either of these well-respected camps of the Lower Zambezi region.

Transfers to Old Mondoro are made from either Sausage Tree or Chiawa by boat, and that alone is a fantastic experience – gliding down the greatest river in southern Africa past herds of elephant and hippo. The energetic and adventurous also have the option of canoeing from either camp to Old Mondoro. Once in camp, walking trails and game drives in open vehicles are on offer. The region is well known for its cats, and the name 'Old Mondoro' is in fact said to derive from a legendary white lion that once roamed these parts.

A typical afternoon at Old Mondoro sees elephants walking into camp.

Guests set off on an afternoon walk through a forest of winterthorns.

Frogs fill in the silence at Old Mondoro's riverside dinners.

During the dry winter months, lion wait for game along the river.

details

When to go
Old Mondoro is open from 1 May to 31 October. The best months for game viewing are July to November, although May and June can be excellent too.

How to get there
There are daily light-aircraft flights from Lusaka to Lower Zambezi's Jeki airstrip. Old Mondoro is then reached by road or river from either Sausage Tree or Chiawa.

Who to contact
Chiawa Camp. Tel (+260-1) 26 1588, e-mail *info@chiawa.com* or go to *www.chiawa.com*. Sausage Tree Camp. Tel. (+260-1) 27 2456, e-mail *info@sausagetreecamp.com* or go to *www.sausagetreecamp.com*

Voted as one of the top tented

camps in Africa, Sausage Tree offers

a refined and romantic experience,

with excellent game viewing.

sausage tree camp

lower zambezi national park

When I first visited Sausage Tree Camp in 1996, it was being run by Jason Mott, a young Australian who had come to southern Africa on a surfing sabbatical. Eight years later, his surfboard is collecting dust in Lusaka and he is now a partner in the camp. Since he has been involved with Sausage Tree Camp, the Lower Zambezi National Park has appeared on the international map and it has been described along with the most stylish tented lodges in the world. With grand white marquee tents, exquisite open-air bathrooms, interesting memorabilia such as old trunks and brass telescopes, and the sort of linen, pillows, glasses and furnishings that you would expect in a luxurious high-street hotel, it's not surprising that Sausage Tree Camp is a sought-after destination.

It is located close to the Chifungulu Channel, a spectacular waterway that bisects the park and provides a stunning stretch of calm water for canoeing. While on the water, any worry that lingers from your everyday life will quickly ebb away as it is quiet and smooth here, and ideal for birdwatching. Other activities on the menu are boat trips, walking trails, fishing, game drives and night drives. Jason maintains that nearly everyone at the camp gets to see lions and about half see leopards. I was lucky enough to see wild dogs too.

Like many great tourist operations, it's a down-to-earth, owner-run business. There's a high degree of service here with personal butlers dedicated to the wishes of each guest, whether they need drinks to be fetched or baths to be run. Another very important member of the Sausage Tree team is Honoré Kabongo, a Congolese, Paris-trained chef who has been lending his culinary skill and delightful charm to the camp for five years.

There's only one creature that has been at Sausage Tree longer than Jason and that's Frank the resident hippo,

on the water, any worry
that lingers from your
everyday life will quickly
ebb away as it is quiet and
smooth here, and ideal
for birdwatching

PREVIOUS SPREAD White-fronted bee-eaters breed in the riverbanks near the lodge.

Elephants frequently cross the river in front of Sausage Tree Camp.

Always concerned about the safety of guests, a canoe guide gives a hippo the right of way.

THIS SPREAD Even the loos are stylish.

The slope of the Zambezi escarpment offers a great view for sunset drinks.

Big game is never far away.

A quiet read on Sausage Tree's deck is often interrupted by hippos, elephant or buffalo.

The Chifungulu Channel offers a quiet and peaceful canoeing and birding experience.

who has been lounging around in front of the camp for as long as anyone can remember. For all this time he's been a loner, so there was some surprise when fellow hippo, Stein, joined him this year. Guests are enjoying the new pairing of Frank 'n Stein, who provide wonderful riverside entertainment. So too do the colourful bee-eaters that nest in the riverbank right at the lodge.

For me, the highlight at Sausage Tree Camp came one blisteringly hot October day, when I found myself on an island of sand in the middle of the Zambezi, with cool water tickling my feet, a freshly prepared Caesar salad on a table, and a waiter standing by with cold beer and wine. This is living large, I thought. And as if that wasn't enough, a herd of elephant slowly wandered by.

Smoother than a game-drive – and just as rewarding – is a sunset cruise on the Zambezi River.

African wild dogs – one of Africa's rarest carnivores – play in the evening light.

Sausage Tree's glorious tents have exquisite views over the Zambezi.

Delicious candle-lit meals are served under the stars on the bank of the river.

Another delicious, and healthy, lunch prepared by the inimitable chef, Honoré Kabongo.

Sausage Tree's romantic baths have great views of the river.

I found myself on an island in the middle of the Zambezi, with cool water tickling my feet

details

When to go
Sausage Tree is open from April to November. The best months for fishing and game viewing are September to November, although April and May can be excellent too.

How to get there
There are daily 40-minute light-aircraft flights from Lusaka to Lower Zambezi National Park's Jeki airstrip. The game drive from there to Sausage Tree can take one to two hours, depending on how much wildlife is seen on the way.

Who to contact
Sausage Tree Camp. Tel. (+260-1) 21 2597, e-mail info@sausagetreecamp.com or go to www.sausagetreecamp.com

kulefu tented camp

lower zambezi national park

One of the easternmost camps
of the Lower Zambezi region,
Kulefu Tented Camp combines luxury
with a traditional bush experience.

With temperatures in the high 30s and low 40s, and skies heavy with dust, I experienced typical October weather for most of my stay in Lower Zambezi National Park. At Kulefu Tented Camp however, the pressure cooker burst and splatters of rain finally fell upon the dusty plains. My hosts were concerned that the dark skies would hamper my experience, but it was quite the opposite. I saw it as a time of renewal, and once the early rains had burnt off, the previously dusty skies were left brilliantly clear. Elephants ceased their continuous ear-flapping and relaxed, and animals that had been languid in the heat became active during the day.

In the space of a day, I went on two short game drives from the camp and was rewarded with memorable sightings of lions, leopards and wild dogs.

Kulefu's fishing opportunities – on a catch-and-release basis for all fish species – are also excellent. One afternoon the resident camp guide, Andrew Ross, took us upstream to a narrow inlet, where we tried our luck at catching fish. Despite my usually poor efforts as a fisherman, I hooked a couple of bream and an impressive tigerfish in the space of 10 minutes. 'That's just the sort of down-to-earth safari experience we like to offer,' said Dave Bennett, who together with John Glendinning runs Star of Africa's safari camps, including Kulefu. 'Kulefu is the most rustic camp on the circuit and we want to keep it that way.'

Star of Africa bought Kulefu as an existing operation, but has since brought in elegant period furniture and natural textiles to give the camp a colonial atmosphere. The living area and dining room are housed in a central marquee, and the eight spacious tented rooms on raised teak decks each have their own en-suite facilities.

After my visit to Kulefu, the big rains arrived and, like other camps in the Lower Zambezi, Kulefu closed up for the season. When it re-opens next year it will be rebuilt, along much the same lines, in a grand new site on the bank of the Zambezi River.

'Kulefu is the most
rustic camp on the
circuit, and we want
to keep it that way'

details

When to go
Kulefu Tented Camp is open from 1 May
to 31 October.

How to get there
There are daily flights from Lusaka to
Lower Zambezi's Jeki airstrip. It's an
hour-and-a-half's drive through the park
from Jeki to Kulefu.

Who to contact
Star of Africa. Tel. (+260-1) 27 1366 or
27 1508/9, fax (+260-1) 27 1398,
e-mail *reservations@starofafrica.co.zm*
or go to *www.star-of-africa.com*

valley of leopards

north & south luangwa national parks

The Mwaleshi River in North Luangwa National Park.

South Luangwa National Park is one of the world's prime game-viewing areas, with spectacular scenery and unusual species such as puku and Thornicroft giraffe, and plenty of leopards. North Luangwa National Park has more of a wilderness feel, with a magnificent escarpment and rivers frequented by buffalo herds and attendant lions.

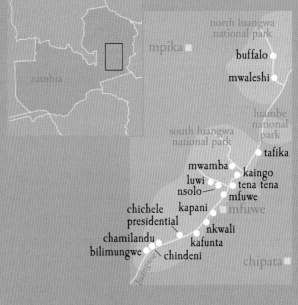

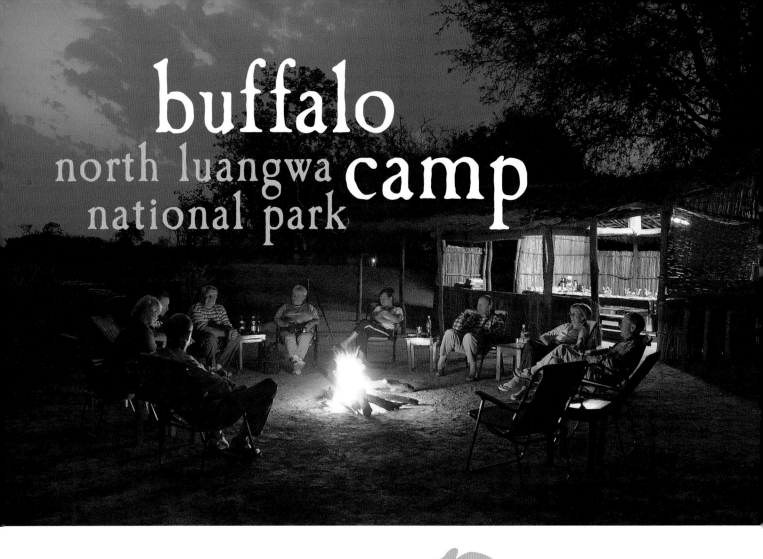

buffalo
north luangwa camp
national park

The first camp to open in North Luangwa enjoys a prime location in a central plain favoured by grazers – and there are plenty of predators too.

Perhaps the most informal of all the camps in Zambia is Buffalo Camp in North Luangwa National Park. Lorna and John Harvey (daughter and son-in-law of the legendary Sir Stewart Gore-Browne of Shiwa Ng'andu Manor; see page 136) established it in 1986, and since their death in 1992 their son Mark has been running it.

Barefoot and quick with a smile and a good sense of humour, Mark offers self-catering or full-board accommodation that ensures a regular flow of dusty independent visitors to the camp. It's a fun scenario, with the chance that you could be dining on fillet steak prepared by Mark's chefs, while a self-catering group dines on bully beef and baked beans. No one seems to mind this though, as the 'game-lodge experience' can be had for a fraction of the normal catered price.

Buffalo Camp offers four double-storey reed chalets on the bank of the Mwaleshi River. Each has a bedroom, flush toilet and shower on the upper floor, with water being heated on a fire below. The Mwaleshi is a shallow, sandy river that is perfect for swimming. But keep a close watch – a herd of buffalo and four adult lions crossed the river metres from where I had swum!

Buffalo Camp has the prime location in North Luangwa, situated in the centre of a plain favoured by grazers. When I visited in 2000 the game was somewhat skittish, but four years on we came very close to kudu, wildebeest, buffalo and even lion. Mark attributes the change to the fine work of the North Luangwa Conservation Project, which has reduced poaching considerably, as well as the increase in positive tourism activity.

Fireside stories at Buffalo Camp are made even more memorable by the roar of a lion or the call of a hyaena.

The wilderness atmosphere in Luangwa has been preserved, with excursions almost entirely on foot.

We encountered this male lion during a game walk, but he moved hastily away.

During the heat of the day, buffalo drink from the Mwaleshi River, near Buffalo Camp.

Hippo pools and swimming holes are divided by a narrow stretch of rocks in the headwaters of the Mwaleshi.

In North Luangwa all activities happen on foot, and it's rare to see another person. There are no local villages and little noise – just tranquillity. 'The wilderness atmosphere is always a sure thing,' said Mark, 'but game viewing isn't guaranteed early in the wet season. By September, however, we regularly see up to 2 000 buffalo in a herd, and lions also come down to the river, so there's plenty of action.' He added, 'It's been like the killing fields recently,' and pointed out a plain that was littered with recent kills.

While you're in North Luangwa, don't miss the opportunity of walking to the headwaters of the Mwaleshi River, which lies deep in miombo forest on the slope of the escarpment. Where else on earth, I wondered, can you swim in a pool with hippos grunting just metres away?

details

When to go
Buffalo Camp is open from 1 June to 1 November.

How to get there
There are daily flights from Lusaka to Mfuwe International Airport. It's a further half-hour flight from Mfuwe to Mwaleshi Airstrip in North Luangwa NP, which is about 30 minutes' drive from Buffalo Camp.

Who to contact
Shiwa Safaris. Tel. (+260-1) 22 9261 or 23 1450, e-mail *reservations@zamsaf.co.zm*, *2mark@bushmail.net*, *gameman@zamnet.zm* or go to *www.shiwasafaris.com*

chichele

Once a private presidential
retreat, then a lodge fallen into
disrepair, Chichele has been
restored to its former glory
by Star of Africa and is now
considered to be the grandest
lodge in South Luangwa.

presidential lodge
& puku ridge tented camp

south luangwa national park

Kenneth Kaunda, who was president of Zambia from 1964 to 1991, had a great affinity for wildlife and he built private retreats for himself in prime locations such as Lake Tanganyika, South Luangwa and the Lower Zambezi.

In 1972 he built Chichele Presidential Lodge on a hilltop in South Luangwa's southern Mfuwe region. It was arguably the prime site in the park and, sitting on his veranda on a clear day, he would have seen the outlines of baobabs and other tall trees against the eastern side of the Muchinga Escarpment. But when Kaunda was voted out of office, Chichele, like many other state-owned assets, fell into decay.

In 2000 the lodge was privatised and Star of Africa set about restoring it to its former presidential glory. This Zambian-owned company has also opened lodges in Livingstone and the Lower Zambezi and Lochinvar national parks, creating the most comprehensive safari circuit in the country. Chichele Presidential Lodge is its largest operation and no expense has been spared in transforming the original site. It has become the grandest lodge in South Luangwa, and a look in the visitors' book confirms that current Zambian president, Levy Mwanawasa, and his entourage are among its recent visitors.

PREVIOUS SPREAD *Amaryllis* flowering in South Luangwa after the first rains of the season.

From the comforts of the luxury tents at Puku Ridge, guests often see puku antelope on the plains.

A room fit for a president at Chichele.

THIS SPREAD Ragged thatch, rough wood, stone and colourful fabrics are hallmarks of Puku Ridge.

Wonderful views greet visitors to Chichele, especially in summer when the skies are clear and the bush is green.

The colonial elegance of Chichele, with its fine furniture and original artworks.

A crocodile and a terrapin warm up in the midday sun.

Thornicroft giraffes joust by slapping each other with their necks.

Kenneth Kaunda had a great affinity for wildlife and he built private retreats for himself in prime locations

Chichele is surrounded by a variety of habitats, including riparian forest, miombo and mopane woodland, and open plains, that can be appreciated during morning and afternoon game drives, guided walks and night drives.

From the moment you walk into Chichele's vast reception area, your senses are dominated by the very view that inspired the president's architects many years ago. There are gracious reception rooms, dining areas, studies and an inviting swimming pool.

The furnishings are elegant and include an impressive collection of original botanical artworks. There are 10 Victorian-style lodges built along the edge of the hillside, all of which offer panoramic views.

One of the best game-viewing regions is the large grassland to the north of the camp called the Kakumbi *dambo*. This fertile valley provides grazing for large numbers of puku and other antelope, zebra and predators including lion, leopard and wild dog.

Star of Africa recently opened a second camp called Puku Ridge Tented Camp, situated on the western side of the *dambo*, with stunning views of the plains. While the architects of Chichele had to retain the original façade of Presidential Lodge, they had a much freer hand with Puku Ridge Tented Camp. It is constructed from a mixture of ragged thatch, stone walls, mopane poles and canvas, which blends into the rocky hillside. The soft furnishings are presented in a mix of natural tones, with zebra stripes and leopard-skin prints that complete the old-world safari atmosphere.

Migration routes south of the lodges have been used by elephants for centuries.

In the heat of the day, the swimming pool brings welcome relief.

Chichele is built on a hill in South Luangwa, and has excellent views of the Mfuwe region.

A lion takes a breather after mating – copulation goes on for days, during which time both animals lose condition.

There is always a friendly waiter nearby, ready to serve you a refreshing drink.

your senses are dominated by the very view that inspired the president's architects many years ago

There are six massive tents, each with full-size double beds and walk-in mosquito nets, overhead fans, dressers, indoor and outdoor showers, sunken baths, and private verandas looking onto the plains. I enjoyed dreamy afternoon siestas under the ticking overhead fans, and at night went to sleep with a breeze, listening to the sounds of hippos crunching on the plains below and the occasional baboon barking at lions patrolling the plains.

I also have fine memories of a bush breakfast of eggs, muffins, orange juice and more, served at a beautifully laid table beneath an umbrella on a quiet bank of the Luangwa River ... and of the delicious multi-course meals and freshly brewed Zambian coffee that were served each evening. But sundowners were the high point of staying at Chichele Presidential Lodge, when we watched the blood-red sun being swallowed by dusty September skies. These were experiences truly fit for a president.

> I enjoyed dreamy afternoon siestas under the ticking overhead fans

Swathes of netting, canvas, crisp fabrics and modern fittings combine with reeds and wooden decking to give the tents at Puku Ridge a distinctive style.

Barbel trapped in the shrinking lagoons result in a fishing frenzy.

Poolside relaxation at Chichele.

Breakfast beside the Luangwa.

Buffalo are a favourite prey of lion and are particularly vulnerable at night.

details

When to go
The lodges are open throughout the year. Game viewing is best from April to October. The rest of the year is wetter so game drives are limited, but the green season brings birdlife, and its own attractions.

How to get there
There are daily flights from Lusaka to South Luangwa's Mfuwe International Airport. Chichele Presidential Lodge is an hour's drive from there.

Who to contact
Star of Africa. Tel. (+260-1) 27 1366, 27 1508/9, fax (+260-1) 27 1398, e-mail *reservations@starofafrica.co.zm* or go to *www.star-of-africa.com*

kafunta river lodge
south luangwa national park

The warmth of the welcome – and of the hot tub – are just two of the attractions of this family-owned lodge on the Luangwa River.

& island bush camp

Kafunta lies on the Luangwa River, where it enjoys spectacular views of the distant escarpment and excellent birdwatching. It is one of the most southerly of South Luangwa's all-weather lodges and during the wet summer season guests can still be driven into the park. In the dry season, the drive is less than a kilometre to the pontoon, which gives direct access to South Luangwa's game-rich central region.

A highlight of Kafunta is the natural aquifer that feeds a constant supply of warm, mineral-rich water from the depths of basalt rock to the lodge's hot spring tub. While sitting in the tub with a glass of orange juice in hand, I could watch elephant, buffalo, kudu and puku, as well as crowned cranes and countless other birds that frequent the wetland.

Another thing that flows warmly and naturally at Kafunta River Lodge is the hospitality of its owners Anke and Ron Cowan, who are experienced travellers and guides from Germany and Australia respectively. One or other of them is always around to make sure that guests are feeling welcomed and at home.

Kafunta has a lush garden with pathways leading to eight comfortable wooden chalets on stilts. The living area is open-plan with a swimming pool, bar, restaurant and dining area overlooking the wetland and the river. The candle-lit meals, supplemented with fresh ingredients grown in the lodge's vegetable gardens, are delicious.

South Luangwa was one of the first national parks in Africa to offer night drives, and the chance

the candle-lit meals, supplemented
with fresh ingredients grown in the lodge's
vegetable gardens, are delicious

PREVIOUS SPREAD On the long and
dusty approach road, guests start
dreaming about the natural hot
springs at Kafunta.

A zebra, washed clean and
invigorated by summer rain.

An African ginger lily in bloom after
the summer rains.

THIS SPREAD Kafunta is a
comfortable 'home base' for safaris
as it is open throughout the year.

During the dry months, the pontoon
is used to access the park.

Kafunta's thatched chalets are
raised up on stilts.

They say that great cooking begins
with great ingredients.

to stay out late searching for nocturnal creatures such as civet, genet, porcupine and leopard is a feature of this park. There are high leopard concentrations here and most guests staying for two nights or more are successful in seeing them.

In 2001 Ron and Anke obtained one of the only island concessions in the Luangwa. Getting to this Island Bush Camp is an adventuresome and somewhat bumpy two-hour drive south of Kafunta to a remote region of South Luangwa. The road eventually pops out of the forest at the river, where a boatman waits to pole you into camp.

Island Bush Camp has four reed chalets with private verandas overlooking the river. As there are no vehicles on the island, walking trails take the place of game drives (which can be done on the mainland). Setting off from the camp every morning and evening with a guide and a scout is very exciting. We came upon pods of hippos contesting their space in the rapidly retreating waters, large colonies of carmine bee-eaters and ever-inquisitive giraffes.

Kafunta is regularly used by Africa Geographic Expeditions and, as many readers of *Africa Geographic* magazine will testify, it offers excellent value for money.

In addition to visiting Island Bush Camp, there are overland trips that head north along the river to Luambe and North Luangwa national parks. To North Luangwa, the expedition includes its own chefs, guides and camp staff, and overnights at Buffalo Camp, which is described on page 66.

Whether you're heading north or south from Kafunta, it's good to know that all expeditions end here, with a welcome as warm as the lodge's hot spring tub.

The shower at Island Bush Camp.

Large flocks of crowned cranes congregate in parts of the Luangwa Valley.

Thornicroft giraffe is found in South Luangwa, but not in North.

Part of the thrill of staying at Island Bush Camp is knowing that it is temporary, being rebuilt at the start of the dry season every year.

details

When to go
Kafunta River Lodge is open throughout the year. Island Bush Camp and Buffalo Camp expeditions are offered from 1 June to 31 October.

How to get there
There are daily flights from Lusaka to South Luangwa's Mfuwe International Airport. Kafunta is a 45-minute drive from there.

Who to contact
Kafunta. Tel. (+260-6) 24 6046 or (+871) 762 068 427 (satellite phone), e-mail *kafunta@super-hub.com* or go to *www.luangwa.com*

mfuwe lodge

& the bushcamp company

south luangwa national park

With a choice of four exclusive bush camps, in addition to the lagoon-facing chalets, one is spoilt for choice when staying in South Luangwa.

I arrived at Mfuwe Lodge
to find its guests lined up
at the lip of the swimming
pool, watching a herd of
elephants drinking in the
lagoon beyond

PREVIOUS SPREAD The animals in the Mfuwe
region are some of the most relaxed in the
park, having become used to vehicles.

Mfuwe Lodge overlooks a lagoon.

THIS SPREAD Elephants have also been known
to walk into reception at Mfuwe Lodge.

A bush camp by name, Chindeni is actually
a semi-permanent tented camp.

A surprise bush breakfast in an
ebony forest near Mfuwe.

South Luangwa was one of the first national
parks to allow private operators to lead
night drives in search of nocturnal animals.

Brown-hooded kingfishers are insectivorous.

I arrived at Mfuwe Lodge to find its guests lined up at the lip of the swimming pool, watching a herd of elephants drinking in the lagoon beyond. Then, just metres from my veranda, there stood a herd of extremely relaxed puku.

'That's nothing,' said director of the lodge, Andy Hogg, showing me photographs of a full-grown elephant cow standing in the middle of the reception area. The picture had been taken during the previous green season when a tree in the nearby garden happened to be in fruit.

Mfuwe Lodge is one of the only permanent lodges within the boundaries of South Luangwa National Park, and game-viewing there is excellent. The leopards are pretty easygoing and there's a good chance of running into resident prides of lion.

Mfuwe has 18 lagoon-facing chalets, spacious public areas and expansive gardens. It offers a fun safari atmosphere and is a great destination for first-time safari-goers. For those seeking more solitude than Mfuwe, there are four smaller sister camps, also run by the Bushcamp Company.

Bush camps are usually temporary in Zambia, being constructed from natural materials at the beginning of each dry season. But Andy told me to expect something different at Mfuwe's sister camps. We drove for two hours, without seeing another vehicle, through a wilderness of miombo woodland before arriving at Chamilandu.

This is probably the most exclusive camp in Luangwa, with just three wooden tree-house chalets perched on stilts on the bank of the river, each with staggering views of the Nchindini Hills. They are more permanent than normal bush camps, with

solid wooden decks, neatly thatched roofs and open-sided rooms that have been tastefully decorated with a combination of wrought iron and brass.

Another 10 kilometres to the south is Chindeni, with its four luxury tents on platforms overlooking an oxbow lagoon and the Nchindini Hills. Even further south is Bilimungwe – a much simpler structure in the typical bush camp tradition, and situated near the shallow Kapamba River, which is safe for a dip. The fourth camp is Kuyenda, made entirely from local materials and run by Phil Berry, who is a guiding institution in Zambia, having worked in South Luangwa for more than 40 years. You couldn't wish for a better guide. The camps have 50 kilometres of exclusive waterfront, so you are assured of a real wilderness experience. Guests are given the opportunity to walk between the camps, but game drives and night drives every evening are also on offer.

'The vehicles always choose independent routes from one another and there is no radio contact about sightings,' Andy told me. At Chamilandu, part of me wished there was. It was about eight in the evening when the four other guests arrived late for dinner, eyes glinting with excitement.

'Leopard?' I asked.

'Yes,' they replied.

'Lion?'

'Yes.'

'Anything else?'

They then switched on their camcorder and showed me 10 minutes of once-in-a-lifetime footage of a honey badger digging into a hive filled with honey.

But the honey badger was just one of the creatures I missed. There have been exceptional wild dog sightings in the region and Andy had the pictures to prove it.

> the four camps have 50 kilometres of exclusive waterfront, so you are assured of a real wilderness experience

The tents at Chindeni look out over an oxbow lake, which swells and shrinks with the season.

The Nchindini Hills provide a dramatic backdrop to an evening cruise at Chamilandu.

The Bushcamp Company's most exclusive bathrooms are at Chamilandu.

The young had already hatched from this dung-beetle ball.

Luangwa becomes lush in summer, when buffalo stand out against the green.

details

When to go
Mfuwe Lodge is open throughout the year. The bush camps are open from 1 June to 31 October.

How to get there
There are daily flights from Lusaka to South Luangwa National Park's Mfuwe International Airport. Mfuwe Lodge is about 45 minutes' drive from there. It's a further two- to three-hour drive through the park to the bush camps.

Who to contact
The Bushcamp Company. Tel. (+260-6) 24 6041 or (+871) 762 280 123 (satellite phone), e-mail info@bushcampcompany.com or go to www.mfuwelodge.com or www.bushcampcompany.com

Founded by the late Norman Carr, who pioneered walking safaris in the Zambian bush, Kapani Lodge and its four sister bush camps uphold the spirit of the Luangwa Valley's conservation legend.

norman carr safaris

south luangwa national park

pods of hippos were wallowing on the distant shores

PREVIOUS SPREAD The Luwi riverbed is great for walking. It's dry for most of the year, and the water that lies in pools draws game from surrounding regions.

THIS SPREAD Immortalised in the biography called *Kakuli*, meaning 'old buffalo', Norman Carr is widely regarded as the father of South Luangwa.

The Luwi River is good wild dog territory – this pack chased a young puku into the waiting jaws of a crocodile.

During the dry season, sunset drinks start early in the Luangwa as the sun sinks into the dust-cloaked horizon.

Each of the raised chalets at the charming Nsolo bush camp has gorgeous views.

An African jacana catches a ride on a hippo at Kapani.

During my first visit to South Luangwa National
Park in 1995 my safari took me to Kapani Lodge
and the home of Norman Carr, the man regarded
as the father of this park. He had lived here for
nearly 50 years, spent many years as its first
warden and earned an MBE from the Queen of
England and the affection of hundreds of
Zambians for his effort.

'This is probably the finest wildlife habitat
remaining in Africa,' he told me, gesturing with
his pipe towards the lagoon. An easterly wind had
banked up a lush green carpet of Nile cabbage
against the nearest bank and pods of hippos were
wallowing on the distant shores. Closer by, aquatic
birds stalked languidly through the viscous brown
water, while elephants and pukus fed quietly on
the lush grassy banks.

Norman Carr, affectionately known as *Kakuli*,
meaning 'old buffalo', passed away in 1996, but
Kapani Lodge, with its elegant colonial atmosphere, expansive lawns, tall avenues of trees and
comfortable chalets, reflects his touch. Many of
the staff were employed by him, his photographs
adorn the walls, and his children are involved in
running the camp. The lodge was built in 1986,
with 10 rooms situated on the fringe of the
Kapani Lagoon. It's a gracious place where teas
are served on a deck overlooking the lagoon and
dinners are served al fresco by the pool, weather
permitting. South Luangwa National Park lies just
across the river and it's a short drive from Kapani
to one of its best game-viewing areas.

Norman believed that the true bush experience
could only be found far away from people, and in
this fine spirit the company offers four bush
camps deep inside the park, away from popular
tourist routes. These camps are freshly built each
season, and despite being simple, they offer great
comforts and excellent cuisine.

I heard that there had been excellent wild dog sightings at Luwi and an alarm call from a puku drew me quickly from my morning tea and toast

Mchenja's five thatched huts are in an ebony grove beside the Luangwa River, with a wonderful hide overlooking a deep lagoon. At Kakuli, five traditional walk-in tents are spectacularly sited at the confluence of the Luangwa and Luwi rivers. The Luwi area offers great walking and game viewing and this is where the other two bush camps, Nsolo and Luwi, are situated. With four spacious chalets built on raised wooden decks and a thatched *chitenge* overlooking a waterhole, Nsolo has a remote and very relaxed atmosphere. Luwi is even simpler, with reed-and-thatch chalets a mere hippo grunt from the Luwi Lagoon.

I heard that there had been excellent wild dog sightings at Luwi and an alarm call from a puku drew me quickly from my morning tea and toast. Sure enough, we found eight wild dogs and a herd of puku running and leaping in all directions in the dry riverbed. One young puku was less experienced at this preservation ritual than the rest however, and darted into the jaws of a crocodile in the Luwi Lagoon!

Watching wild dogs on foot... I felt sure Norman Carr would have approved. It felt strange to come to South Luangwa without paying my respects to this legendary man so, on my last day at Kapani, I was shown to the ebony forest where he used to enjoy picnics with his family.

Here, hat in hand, I read the words on a small monument: 'Norman Carr, Conservationist, 1912–1996. May he rest in peace here in the quiet of the park, which will forever be his monument.'

Bush camp décor at Luwi Camp
includes natural textures and
African fabrics.

Yellow-billed storks fly in to join a
fishing party in the Luangwa.

Tea at Kapani is served on this deck,
at the edge of a lagoon.

The Luwi Lagoon.

details

When to go
Kapani is open throughout the year.
The bush camps are open from 1 June
to 31 October.

How to get there
There are daily flights from Lusaka to
Mfuwe International Airport. From here
it's a 45-minute drive to Kapani.

Who to contact
Norman Carr Safaris.
Tel. (+260-6) 24 6015, e-mail
kapani@normancarrsafaris.com
or go to *www.normancarrsafaris.com*

remote africa safaris

south & north luangwa national parks

From the Coppinger family's

four camps you can explore

South and North Luangwa

national parks on foot, by

game-drive vehicle, canoe

and even microlight.

When John and Carol Coppinger built their five-chalet camp under giant leadwood trees on a bend of the Luangwa River in the northern Nsefu Sector, they called it *Tafika*, meaning 'we have arrived'.

'We like to think we are unpretentious,' says John. 'This is our home – we brought up our children here – and when guests come we want them to feel like part of the family. We are straight-down-the-line people and want to offer a real bush experience, but with good food, and comforts such as down pillows.'

Tafika really does feel like home. Guests enjoy three excellent meals a day with the family and are free to help themselves to drinks from the fridges. Full breakfasts are served around the fire overlooking the Luangwa each morning before game drives. Lunches are sit-down affairs in the *chitenge*, accompanied by crisp salads harvested from the vegetable garden, and multi-course dinners are served under starry skies.

For one American family I met, the highlight of their stay was visiting Tafika's community project. Last year John and Carol raised $7 400 from guests to subsidise teachers' wages, finance promising students and build a clinic. 'It's a way of making local people enjoy tourism,' says John.

John has worked in the Luangwa Valley for more than 21 years, and others in his team have worked for 30. It goes without saying that the guided walks, game drives and night drives are of the highest standard. 'We are very lucky to be in this region,' said John. 'It's remote and has access to a mix of riparian forest, saltpans and wide, open plains. There are plenty of leopards, large herds of buffalo

PREVIOUS SPREAD A guide shows guests the fleshy fruit of a sausage tree, which is used in cream for skin disorders.

Tafika, which means 'we have arrived', is the home of the Coppinger family.

A hyaena cub with its mother in the Nsefu Sector of South Luangwa National Park.

THIS SPREAD Luangwa's shrinking lagoons are the focal point for game activity during the dry months.

If you're careful of crocs, the Mwaleshi River is shallow enough to cross.

A large herd of buffalo.

Tafika's homely and welcoming lounge.

It's a short flight and an exciting drive to Mwaleshi in North Luangwa.

'when guests come we want them to feel like part of the family'

and we often come across lion. There is also a spectacular breeding colony of yellow-billed storks and a large concentration of crowned cranes.'

John used to be a commercial pilot and now keeps up his flying by assisting Zambian Wildlife Authority and taking guests on 15-minute flights in his microlight. Flying offers a great opportunity to get an aerial perspective of the river, with its massive pods of hippos choking the channels and big herds of buffalos.

Game viewing in the region peaks in the dry season when the waters recede. At this time, John opens his walking trail camps in the national park. Chikoko, which was one of the first walking camps set up in Luangwa, overlooks a lagoon and features double-storey rooms with bedrooms upstairs and bathrooms below. Crocodile Camp lies in a grove of mahogany trees near a string of lagoons that attract plenty of game. There are no roads to these camps and this adds greatly to their remoteness. All the walking camps are rustic, but they are also very comfortable, with shower water heated on the fire and food prepared to the same high standard as at the main lodge.

Mwaleshi Camp, which lies in North Luangwa, feels even more isolated and relaxed. Here, four simple reed chalets are strung along a bank of the shallow Mwaleshi River near the confluence with the Luangwa. This is spectacular walking country and the chances of seeing lion and buffalo are excellent, particularly late in the dry season.

When the rains start to fall in late November the walking trail camps are packed away until the dry season, but John then busies himself with river safaris on the flooded river from Tafika, and he also leads exciting multi-day expeditions that head to the source of the Luangwa.

John Coppinger gives an aerial introduction to South Luangwa while flying guests by microlight over the Luangwa River.

Pods of hippos are often seen from the microlight.

Crocodile Camp and its sister camp Chikoko are in a walking-only section of South Luangwa.

The walking camps are rustic but comfortable.

flying offers a great opportunity to get an aerial perspective of the river, with its massive pods of hippos choking the channels

details

When to go
Tafika is operated seasonally, from 15 May to 30 November and 10 February to 10 April. Chikoko is open from 15 May to 31 October and Crocodile from 1 June to 31 October. Mwaleshi is open from 15 June to 31 October. River safaris are offered from 10 February to 10 April.

How to get there
Tafika is a two-hour drive from Mfuwe Airport and 10 minutes from Lukuzi Airstrip. Crocodile and Chikoko bush camps can both be reached on foot in an hour, with porters carrying bags. Mwaleshi Airstrip is a half-hour flight north and it's a 15-minute drive, or 45-minute walk to camp.

Who to contact
Remote Africa Safaris.
E-mail *tafika@remoteafrica.com*
or go to *www.remoteafrica.com*

robin pope safaris

south luangwa national park

Robin Pope Safaris, which has an inimitable reputation in South Luangwa,

has three camps in the valley and also offers fly-camping and guided

walking trails.

Robin is regarded
as one of the best
walking guides
in Africa and
Robin Pope
Safaris is one of
the most success-
ful operations in
Luangwa

PREVIOUS SPREAD Tena Tena is the flagship camp of Robin Pope Safaris.

During the dry season, sausage tree flowers are a tasty treat for most antelope.

Puku are the most widespread of the antelope in South Luangwa.

THIS SPREAD On a walking safari, expert guides show trailists how to creep up on animals safely.

Tena Tena's tents are rich in colour and comfort, and they even have electrical points for charging batteries.

Nkwali offers a boat trip followed by a game drive, which treats guests to an exciting 'river and park' experience.

The Luangwa River runs between Nkwali and the national park.

Nsefu was the first private camp to open in the park – and its historical character has been retained.

In 1974 **Robin Pope asked** the man who pioneered the first walking trails in South Luangwa, Norman Carr, for some work.

'What bird is that?' asked Norman as a yellow-billed stork flew by. Robin thought such an easy question must be a joke, and chuckled in reply. The story goes that he didn't get the job and it wasn't until the following year that a group of pipe-smoking hunters walked with him around a lagoon, became impressed with his knowledge, and then proclaimed him a guide.

Today Robin is regarded as one of the best walking guides in Africa and Robin Pope Safaris is one of the most successful operations in Luangwa. It consists of an all-weather camp at Nkwali, two dry-season camps in the Nsefu Sector, as well as walking and fly-camping safari operations. Much of the credit for their success goes to Robin's wife Jo, herself a zoologist, whose marketing skill and dedication is legendary in the valley. She has long championed the international marketing of South Luangwa and is now a director of a brand-new scheduled airline, Airwaves Airlink.

I met up with Jo and Robin at Nkwali, a six-chalet camp near Mfuwe, which also serves as their home and the base for their operation. From the veranda, we watched the sun setting in the dust-filled skies and hippos yawning at the night.

'Walking is like reading a book and game drives are like films,' Robin told me, quoting the words of one of the guests who had been on a previous trail. 'Four times a year, I take expeditions to remote regions of Luangwa, and because I'm a bit of a generalist, we spend five days enjoying a good walk, covering between 50 and 70 kilometres and learning a bit about everything.

'We like to keep our camps simple and down to earth,' he added. 'And there must always be a view into nature.'

I stayed one night at Nkwali in a stunning brick-and-thatch chalet, which was set a few metres back from the steep sides of the Luangwa River. Even though I could see elephants and hippos from my bed, I was drawn to morning and afternoon game drives in South Luangwa National Park, which we reached via the hand-drawn Nkwali pontoon. Because Nkwali is open for nine months of the year, it's an ideal base for anyone wanting to visit the park during the wet, green season.

Robin's House, which is a self-contained five-bedded unit with its own staff, is also available to hire.

Robin Pope Safaris runs two camps in the Nsefu Sector, a remote region inside the park which is only open for five

Leopards in Luangwa – and there are plenty of them – are most frequently sighted at dusk or at night.

Fly-camps capture the spirit of a traditional safari.

A walking party stops for a hilltop view of South Luangwa National Park.

Nsefu may be historical, but there's nothing dated about the camp's stylish interiors.

'We like to keep
our camps
simple and
down to earth,'
he added.
'And there must
always be a view
into nature.'

The chirping of parrots leads birders to a sausage tree.

Carmine bee-eaters amass in the Nsefu Sector during October.

A fly-camp shower is a welcome sight after a hot and dusty day on foot.

All the animals, including elephants, seem more settled during the abundance of the summer season.

months of the year during the dry winter season.

One of these camps is Nsefu, which was actually the first tourism camp to open in Zambia, when Norman Carr brokered a deal with the local chief in 1951. Robin's roots in the camp are strong because he ran it for five years between 1979 and 1984, and then bought and re-opened it in 1999, retaining the original rondavels in the new camp design. Nsefu's setting is stunning, with views up and down the river and a waterhole that is well-visited by game. Sitting in the *chitenge*, I watched seven mammal species arriving to drink, and hundreds of carmine bee-eaters nesting in the banks.

The other camp is Tena Tena, which opened 12 kilometres downstream in 1985, and is the flagship camp of the Robin Pope Safaris operation. Its four luxurious tents, complete with Persian carpets and open-air bathrooms, represent the pinnacle of understated elegance in the valley.

Both Nsefu and Tena Tena are situated in an extremely game-rich region with

spectacular lagoons and large grassland plains. These surround some natural springs, which attract crowned cranes by the thousand.

I went walkabout in Nsefu with Deb Tittle, who runs the fly-camping division and is regarded as one of the best guides in the valley. After spending much of the day sneaking up on elephants and buffalos, we eventually walked into our camp, which had been set up on an open plain under a solitary tree, next to a drying lagoon.

With the dust and sweat of the day having been washed off by a warm bucket-shower, we settled down for a fireside chat. 'The beauty of fly-camping is that before we arrive it's all virgin bush and when we leave it's the same as it was before,' Deb told us. 'The animals have no time to become accustomed to us and their curiosity wins as they go about their normal business.'

I fell asleep comfortably, on a mattress on the ground, listening to the sounds of owls, leopards and baboons filtering through the canvas of my tent.

I fell asleep ...
listening to the
sounds of owls,
leopards and
baboons

details

When to go
Nkwali and Robin's House are open
from April to December. Tena Tena
and Nsefu are open from June to
October. Mobile safaris are offered
from mid-June to September and
fly-camping from June to October.

How to get there
Mfuwe International Airport is
45 minutes by road from Nkwali,
70 minutes from Tena Tena and
90 minutes from Nsefu.

Who to contact
Robin Pope Safaris. Tel. (+260-6)
24 6090, fax (+260-6) 24 6094,
e-mail *info@robinpopesafaris.net*
or go to *www.robinpopesafaris.net*

With two camps and four superb hides, Derek Shenton's operation is appreciated by nature-lovers and wildlife photographers, who come back again and again.

shenton safaris

south luangwa national park

I've returned several times to Kaingo since my first visit in 1995. I have watched flocks of birds devour barbel from shrinking lagoons, seen vast herds of Cookson's wildebeest and Thornicroft giraffe, and been in the presence of lions, buffalos and leopards aplenty.

Derek Shenton, who built and runs Kaingo, has a close affinity with nature, and this adds to the atmosphere of the camp. It's not surprising that his father, Barry, used to be a ranger in Luangwa and the warden of Kafue National Park.

'It's a privilege to be in a national park,' said Derek. 'This is a very old valley – about 150 million years – and we must look after it. We take out all our rubbish and assist national parks by grading roads and improving infrastructure. We also support anti-poaching and privately fund patrols. Our impact is very low, and one of the benefits is having animals – even leopard – come right into camp.'

Kaingo lies on a quiet stretch of river opposite South Luangwa's game-rich Nsefu Sector. In addition to the area's beautiful river vistas there is a three-square-kilometre ebony forest, which is one of the largest in the park and just a short drive from Kaingo.

'Those ebonies were mature when Livingstone walked through this reserve,' observed Derek as we enjoyed sundowners on the fringe of the forest one evening.

Kaingo is a great spot for game viewing. Lots of elephants and baboons take refuge here in the dappled cool and feed on the fruits of the ebony trees. 'We have two prides of lion in this area of the park, and leopards, which nine out of 10 of our guests get to see,' he added.

Extending out over the river is a viewing platform from which you can see hippos and elephants. At midday, when the cicadas are chirping and most of the game is hiding, you can delay a traditional afternoon siesta and head upstream to a hippo hide built into a bank at the confluence of the Luangwa and Mwamba rivers. With some 200 hippos heaving, snarling and yawning just metres away from where you sit, all thoughts of sleep will vanish.

Active all year is the Mwamba Last Waterhole hide, which becomes more spectacular as the season progresses. It's a great place to sit and watch all varieties of thirsty game coming to drink.

There is also an elephant hide, high up in an ebony tree on an old migration route, just a short distance from camp. From late August a mobile bird hide is moored near the colonies of carmine bee-eaters, and this provides great viewing of these colourful migrants at dawn and dusk, as they build their nests into the banks of the river.

Kaingo has five unpretentious brick-and-thatch chalets on the edge of the

delay a traditional
afternoon siesta and
head upstream to a
hippo hide

Luangwa River. One of these is the romantic honeymoon suite, which has a skylight for star-gazing and an outdoor bath perched on the edge of the river. The camp owes much of its character to the Shenton family, who supply homemade soaps, batiks and fresh produce from their vegetable plot outside the park. It's also quiet here, with solar power instead of generators, and a hippo chorus as the only distraction.

Three hours' walk (or a 20-minute drive) from Kaingo lies Mwamba, an even more remote and peaceful camp in a superb game-viewing area, with wide, open plains, woodlands and walks along the Mwamba River. The nearby Lion Plain supports big buffalo herds, Cookson's wildebeest and a pride of six lionesses and two impressive dark-maned males.

Shenton Safaris' return rate of six out of 10 guests – and I am one of them – speaks for itself. 'Most of our guests have special interests or are very keen photographers,' said Derek.

The ebony forest near Kaingo is one of the largest in the valley.

Many hippos bear scars inflicted by formidable tusks.

Hippo-viewing from the hippo hide.

Mwamba's bar is a great place to share 'bush stories'.

Puku drop their young throughout the year.

DEREK SHENTON

it's also quiet here, with solar power instead of generators, and a hippo chorus as the only distraction

details

When to go
Kaingo and Mwamba are both
open during the dry season. Kaingo
opens 20 May, Mwamba opens
1 June to the end of October.

How to get there
There are daily flights from
Lusaka to South Luangwa's Mfuwe
International Airport. Kaingo is
a two-hour drive from there,
90 minutes of which is through
the park. Mwamba is a three-hour
walk or a 20-minute vehicle transfer from Kaingo.

Who to contact
Shenton Safaris. Tel. (+260-6)
24 5064, e-mail *info@kaingo.com*
or go to *www.kaingo.com*

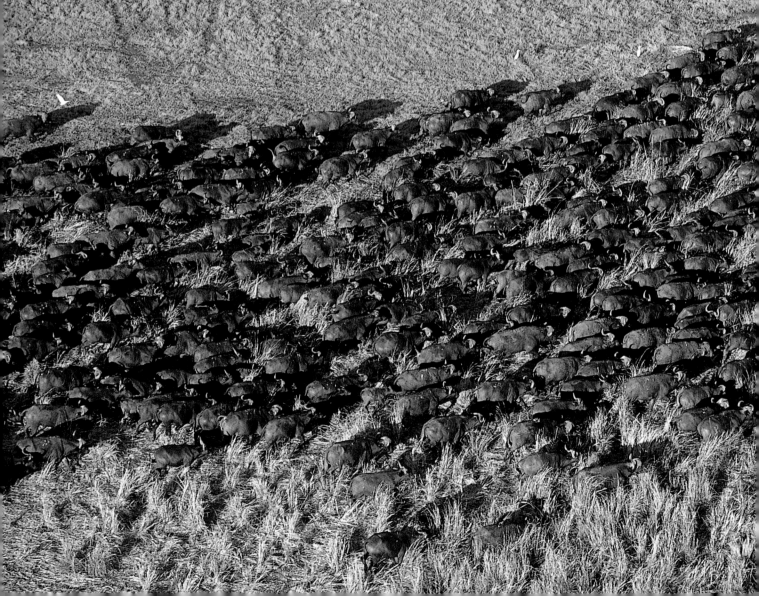

highlands of plenty
kafue and the central highlands

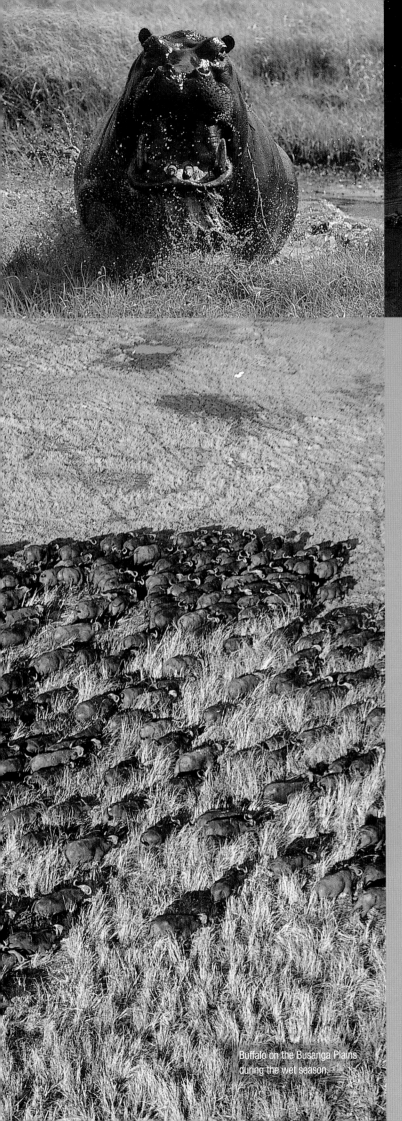

Buffalo on the Busanga Plains during the wet season.

Most of Zambia lies on a vast, high-lying plateau covered by miombo woodland. Kafue National Park, with its wide rivers and vast plains, is one of the most diverse regions. Another gem is Lochinvar National Park, with its wetland of international importance.

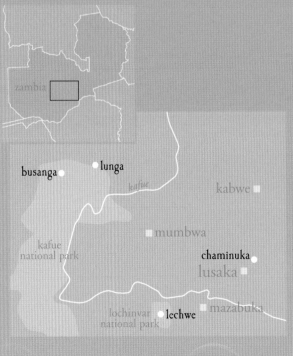

zambia

busanga   lunga   kafue   kabwe

kafue
national park   mumbwa

chaminuka

lusaka

lochinvar   lechwe   mazabuka
national park

chaminuka lodge
lusaka

Promoting Zambian art is as much an interest of the owners of this private nature reserve as preserving the wildlife in it. Works of distinguished artists adorn the walls, while a variety of animals roam the surrounds.

Chaminuka Lodge is built on a hill in a private nature reserve outside Lusaka, with panoramic views over Lake Chitoka and miombo woodland and savanna. It's an unusual sort of place that piques your curiosity about what makes its owners tick, and mine was satisfied when a smallish man with a shock of white hair and penetrating eyes marched towards me and introduced himself as the owner.

'My name is Andrew Sardanis,' he said, 'and this is my family home.'

Andrew arrived in Zambia more than 50 years ago as a young journalist from Cyprus and, with a Zambian partner, developed a chain of trading stores throughout the country. During the 1960s he became increasingly influential in Zambia both as a businessman and as a close friend of former Zambian president Kenneth Kaunda and a member of his administration.

In the late 1970s Andrew built his home at Chaminuka, and settled there with his wife Danae and their two sons Stelios and Harry.

The name 'Chaminuka' means 'small hill' or 'hump' and derives from a village in north-western Zambia where Andrew lived as a young man.

The lodge is inspired by the design of an African village, with several *insakas* (airy lounge areas) where guests can relax and enjoy the views. It is well regarded for its fine dining, attentive service and luxurious rooms that have been decorated with original paintings and statues.

PREVIOUS SPREAD Chaminuka Lodge, brilliant under the indigo blue of the African night sky.

Giraffes are often seen during game drives.

THIS SPREAD Numerous hunting trophies and works of art reflect the family's history and interests.

Driving through miombo woodland, you will come across giraffe, eland, sable and many other animals of the Zambian bush.

The walls of the lodge are decorated with works of art collected in Zambia and other parts of Africa.

Chaminuka fits into its surroundings and becomes part of them, and the landscape, the horizon and the sky above are extensions of the interior.

the lodge is inspired by the design of an African village, with several *insakas* where guests can relax

'Chaminuka has helped shape art in Zambia and Zambian art has helped shape Chaminuka'

Chaminuka is most revealing about the Sardanises' life and their love for art and nature. The walls and rooms are decorated with hundreds of works of art, modern and traditional, collected in Zambia and many other parts of Africa over the past five decades. On the walls you can trace the progress of distinguished artists such as Patrick Mumba, Petson Lombe, Henry Tayali and Godfrey Setti, and sculptor Flinto Chandia.

'Chaminuka has helped shape art in Zambia and Zambian art has helped shape Chaminuka,' Stelios commented. 'But most of all it is the people,' writes Andrew in his book *Africa: Another side of the coin*, 'that shaped Chaminuka.'

Stelios took me on a tour of the property and showed me the churches, the two schools and the village decorated with colourful murals painted by street kids and children from the villlage. Stelios also showed me the Kaposhi Cheese Factory that he runs, and where he takes guests on cheese-tasting tours.

Chaminuka was, in 1979, the first private nature reserve to be registered in Zambia and it is also the country's largest. It comprises pristine miombo woodland savanna and lakes and offers a startling array of wildlife, including buffalo, elephant, giraffe, sable, hartebeest, wildebeest and zebra, not to mention the prolific diversity of birdlife. Guests are able to go on walks and game drives through the reserve.

The Chaminuka Bushcamp is set well away from the lodge, and on my last evening I was invited to join the Sardanis family for dinner and some music. 'It's going to be a party,' one of the Zambian waiters told me – and so it was!

After a meal cooked on the open fire, five resident musicians entertained our group with all manner of instruments, including one that doubled as a guitar and drum. I've heard many excellent staff 'singalongs' at lodges throughout Africa, but the soulful artistry of those from Chaminuka will remain longest in my memory.

Luxurious outdoor living is a treat for the guests of Chaminuka Lodge.

The rooms have hotel comforts including telephones, fridges and air-conditioning.

The murals in the village were painted by street kids as well as children from the villlage.

The Chaminuka Bushcamp is set well away from the lodge.

details

When to go
Chaminuka is open throughout the year.

How to get there
Chaminuka is a 20-kilometre drive from Lusaka International Airport.

Who to contact
Chaminuka. The lodge: Tel. (+260-1) 21 3303/4/5. The Lusaka office (+260-1) 22 2694/22 5432, e-mail *reservations@chaminuka.com* or go to *www.chaminuka.com*

lechwe plains

Countless bird species and thousands of Kafue lechwe put on a wonderful show at Lechwe Plains – the only game lodge in the spectacular Lochinvar National Park.

tented camp
lochinvar national park

At Lochinvar National Park, the Kafue River empties itself over a massive wetland of several thousand hectares, known as the Kafue Flats. Here the flooded grassy plains, still waters and smoke-grey skies seem to melt together like giant slabs of polished slate. The shallow waters support over 400 bird species, while the seasonally flooded grasslands and woodlands are strongholds for massive herds of the endemic Kafue lechwe, and buffalo, zebra and oribi.

Within Lochinvar National Park, Star of Africa has built a superb tented camp on the shores of the Chunga Lagoon. It has an open-sided dining tent that is decorated in colonial style with fine dark wood furniture, comfortable chairs and antique rugs. Six double tents, which cater for a total of 12 guests at any one time, are situated alongside the lagoon.

In the evenings we explored the famous Lechwe Plains in an open-topped game-viewing vehicle and watched herds of zebra thundering across the horizon. As the early morning mist rose off the lagoon, we glided in *mekoro* just 50 metres from herds of Kafue lechwe, which occur here in the tens of

thousands. We also saw several interesting waterbirds such as wattled cranes, spoonbills, sandpipers, godwits, avocets, ducks and geese. Summers are particularly rewarding for birdwatchers, with many migrants arriving, including flamingos and pelicans.

Lochinvar National Park has been a RAMSAR Wetland of International Importance since 1991, but in the '70s and '80s the wetland suffered when two major dams were built on the Kafue River. Since then, Star of Africa, WWF and Lochinvar National Park have formed the Partners for Wetlands project, and regular patrols have been established, lechwe- and bird-hunting have been stopped, roads are being upgraded and water is released from the Itezhi-Tezhi Dam to emulate the natural flooding regime of the wetland by the river.

Star of Africa is also raising funds through its Community Development Projects Division to assist a school in the local fishing village, which will benefit both the local community and the national park.

PREVIOUS SPREAD From the dining tent, there's a great view of the goings-on at the lake.

Lochinvar supports more than 400 bird species, including vast flocks of pelicans, African skimmers and crowned cranes.

A welcome greeting from the friendly staff at Lechwe Plains.

THIS SPREAD Kafue lechwe are found in their thousands, and when they run through water it's as loud as a waterfall.

The marquee-shaped suites are spacious.

Birders can explore the seasonally flooded wetlands by *mokoro*.

Simple things – like bread cooked in a ground oven – make the camp feel like home.

Star of Africa is involved in the local community, and is assisting a school in the fishing village.

the flooded grassy plains, still waters and
smoke-grey skies seem to melt together
like giant slabs of polished slate

details

When to go
Lechwe Plains Tented Camp is open throughout the year. The best time for birding is during the summer months from December to April.

How to get there
From Lusaka it's a half-hour flight to Lochinvar followed by an hour's drive to Lechwe Plains Tented Camp. Alternatively, it's a four-hour drive from Lusaka. Either way, be prepared for a bumpy ride on rutted roads.

Who to contact
Star of Africa. Tel. (+260-1) 27 1366, 27 1508/9, fax (+260-1) 27 1398, e-mail *reservations@starofafrica.co.zm* or go to *www.star-of-africa.com*

lunga river lodge &

busanga bushcamp

kafue national park

The extraordinary biodiversity of
Kafue National Park can be discovered
from Lunga River Lodge and its satellite
camp, Busanga.

I arrived at Kafue National Park's Busanga Plains soon after the first summer rains of 2004, when the grasses covering the plain were lush and green. Nothing had prepared me for the sight – black arum lilies poked above the ground and thousands of tiny blue and white flowers stood out against the green of the grass which stretched to the horizon in each direction. Our sightings of game were spectacular too, with roan antelope and vast herds of red lechwe and buffalo that surpass anything else I have seen in Zambia. There were plenty of lions resting in the trees, no doubt avoiding the sodden ground, and we watched cheetahs keeping vigil from the tops of termite mounds.

For more than 10 years, South African-born Ed Smyth has run Lunga River Lodge in the northern part of Kafue National Park and has been treating guests to his bush camp on the spectacular Busanga Plains. Ed is something of a perfectionist and, despite the fact that his camps are more than 10 hours' drive from even the nearest decent supermarket in Lusaka, every year he manages to refine them, as well as the menus and the experience, into something even more notable than the previous year's.

Busanga Bushcamp is constructed of canvas and natural materials and is rebuilt every year at the start of the rainy season. Ed had a hand in making much of its furniture, from beautifully crafted wooden tables to elegant wrought-iron beds.

the camp at Busanga is constructed
of canvas and natural materials and is
rebuilt every year

PREVIOUS SPREAD Buffalo stampede
across the spectacular green Busanga
Plains.

THIS SPREAD The Lunga River, on whose
bank the lodge is situated, flows slowly off
the escarpment and ultimately into the
Zambezi.

Despite being 10 hours' drive from the
nearest town, the African Experience team
prides itself on providing fresh fruit and
salad, as well as creature comforts.

Busanga is excellent for cats. In addition to
cheetah, sightings of lion and serval are
common.

A black arum lily pokes above the plains
after the first summer rains.

Lunga River Lodge exceeded my expectations with its swimming pool, open bar and balcony suspended over the Lunga River. It was completely rebuilt in 2004 and its small cottages now all have private verandas over-looking the river and spanking new interiors with immaculately tiled floors, neatly thatched roofs and walk-in mosquito nets.

The Lunga River rises in the Democratic Republic of Congo and makes its way south before meeting the Kafue, and finally the Zambezi. It is navigable for only about 10 kilometres before the first rapids begin, and canoeing and birdwatching are sublime experiences here. Bird species such as African finfoot, African skimmer, Ross's turaco, Böhm's bee-eater and western-banded snake eagle are promising lifers for any serious birder's list. Elephant and lion are commonly seen in the area, which is also known for its sable antelope.

Both Lunga and Busanga offer visitors a wonderful base from which to explore Kafue National Park. At more than 22 000 square kilometres, Kafue is larger than Kruger, and with over 480 bird and 150 mammal species, including many specials, it is not to be missed by serious lovers of nature.

the Lunga is navigable for only about 10 kilometres before the first rapids begin, and canoeing here is a sublime experience

Guests staying at Lunga River Lodge can go birding along channels that run off the main stream.

During the wet season the Busanga is inundated with water and it becomes impossible to move around by vehicle.

Most of the exquisite furniture at Lunga River Lodge was made on site by Ed and his team.

The deck overlooking the Lunga River provides a great vantage point for birdwatching.

An enraged hippo guards its small shrinking patch at Busanga Plains.

details

When to go
Lunga and Busanga are open between June and November.

How to get there
Lunga is an hour's flight from Lusaka (Lunga's private airstrip is serviced by Lunga Air Shuttle). It's a further three-hour drive to Busanga.

Who to contact
African Experience. Tel. (+873) 762 093 985 (satellite phone) between May and November or e-mail *info@experienceafrica.com*

into the north
bangweulu region

Some 30 000 black lechwe occur in the Bangweulu Swamps.

In Zambia's north-eastern highlands you will find the sprawling Bangweulu Wetland with its famous shoebill storks, and Kasanka National Park, which is one of the best places in Africa to see sitatunga. Also in the north is Shiwa Ng'andu, an extraordinary mansion in the midst of the African bush.

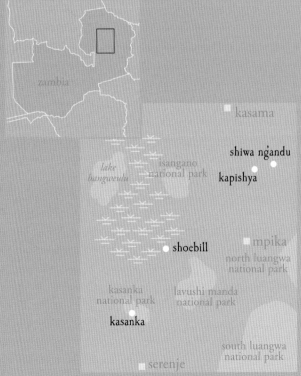

zambia

kasama

shiwa ng'andu

lake bangweulu

isangano national park

kapishya

shoebill

mpika

north luangwa national park

kasanka national park

lavushi manda national park

kasanka

south luangwa national park

serenje

kapishya

northern zambia

Kapishya is about 20 kilometres away from Shiwa Ng'andu and it was here, on the banks of the Manashya River and in the shade of raffia palms and combretums, that Sir Stewart Gore-Browne and his wife Lorna used to spend their holidays. She was a 'ravishing' young lady from England who was nearly 20 years his junior.

The most romantic thing about this quiet little retreat is the natural hot spring that bubbles up from the river at a 'perfect' temperature. The pool is shallow, with a sandy bottom, and is so inviting that people stay in it for hours.

Kapishya today has a string of five delightful cottages that overlook the river. They are relatively inexpensive and offer comfortable rooms, hot water and a team of helpful staff to cook meals. Many of the old-timers who work here can still tell stories about the days of Sir Stewart, otherwise known as *Chipembele* – you can read more about him on page 136.

Kapishya is also the home of Mark Harvey (Sir Stewart's youngest grandson), who is a fascinating character and a great wilderness guide. His company, Shiwa Safaris, also owns Buffalo Camp (see page 66) in North Luangwa, which is a few hours' drive from the hot springs.

After an exciting day's walk in the bush, there can be no better place than Kapishya's hot spring to wash off the dust.

With its hot spring, relaxed style and rustic hospitality, Kapishya is a convenient base from which to visit Shiwa Ng'andu and other attractions of the north.

Warm water bubbles up through white sands into this crystal-clear pool.

The cottages are set in an attractive garden on the bank of the Manashya River.

The family-sized cottages have bedrooms both upstairs and down.

Kapishya's garden is alive with colour and beauty.

There are always good stories to be heard at Kapishya – a fascinating melting pot for travellers moving through northern Zambia.

details

When to go
Kapishya is open throughout the year. Buffalo Camp, which is well combined with a visit to Kapishya, is open from 1 June to 1 November.

How to get there
Air charters fly guests from Lusaka or Mfuwe to Shiwa Ng'andu's airstrip. From Lusaka it's a 12-hour drive to Kapishya.

Who to contact
Shiwa Safaris. Tel. (+260-1) 22 9261 or 23 1450, e-mail *reservations@zamsaf.co.zm*, *2mark@bushmail.net*, *gameman@zamnet.zm* or go to *www.shiwasafaris.com*

shiwa ng'andu

The manor house that was built by Sir Stewart Gore-Browne, and immortalised in the best-selling book *Africa House*, has been renovated by his family and is now open to guests.

Sir Stewart Gore-Browne first saw Shiwa Ng'andu (meaning 'Lake of the Royal Crocodile') in 1914 on a return journey home to England, after serving a stint with the British Colonial Boundary Commission. It was here, in remote northern Zambia, that he decided he would one day build his dream home. In 1920, after serving in World War I, he returned to Shiwa and over the next 40 years he built his home and filled it with silver, china, books, furniture and other items befitting an English gentleman.

By 1925 he had employed 1 000 local people and built schools, a hospital, several workshops and neat rows of quaint red-brick staff and guest cottages with tiled roofs that reflected 'a little piece of England'.

Gore-Browne's determination, and temper, earned him the name Chipembele, meaning 'rhinoceros', and he played an influential role in leading Zambia on the road to independence.

Respected both in England and in Zambia, Gore-Browne died in 1967 and was given a full state funeral by

An unusual marriage between Victorian and Tuscan architecture, the manor house at Shiwa Ng'andu seems out of place in the Zambian bush.

You'll find books on poetry, orchid-growing, colonial history and other interesting subjects in the old library.

After an energetic outride, horses graze in front of Shiwa Lake.

Dignified habits of English gentry are still maintained in the dining room.

Master of the manor, Charlie Harvey, is Sir Stewart Gore-Browne's grandson.

Zambian president, Kenneth Kaunda. He remains the first and only Englishman ever to have earned this honour. As the president said, 'He was born an Englishman and died a Zambian.'

Charlie Harvey (Gore-Browne's eldest grandson) and his wife Jo have renovated the house in recent years and it is now open to paying guests to enjoy its special magic. Guests have undivided and personal attention and can enjoy game drives, horse-riding, boating on Shiwa Lake, candle-lit dinners and access to Gore-Browne's archives. Day trips to nearby Kapishya can also be arranged.

Staying at Shiwa Ng'andu provides an unusual and fascinating insight into Zambia's colonial history.

details

When to go
Shiwa is open throughout the year. It is best combined with a tour of Kasanka, Bangweulu or North Luangwa.

How to get there
Air charters fly guests from Lusaka or Mfuwe to Shiwa Ng'andu's airstrip. From Lusaka, it's a 10-hour drive to Shiwa.

Who to contact
C & J Harvey. Tel. (+260-1) 22 9261, 22 0747, (+260-4) 37 0134 or (+260-97) 74 9002, or e-mail *gameman@zamnet.zm* or *2gameman@bushmail.net* or go to *www.shiwangandu.com*

kasanka national
park bangweulu area

Kasanka, which is run by a private trust, supports conservation in Zambia by enabling visitors to explore its wide range of habitats and the spectacular Bangweulu Swamps.

Kasanka became a national park in 1972, having been protected as a game reserve from as far back as 1946. In 1990 it then became the first national park to be independently managed when the government signed a management agreement with Kasanka Trust. Up to that time there had been no development and the park had suffered from uncontrolled poaching, but the Kasanka Trust has since turned things around through careful management of resources and appropriate development.

Kasanka is now a gem of a park, covering 390 square kilometres of miombo woodland, dry evergreen forest, swamp forest, papyrus swamps, grassy *dambos* and riparian forests, which together support an exceptional diversity of species.

It is one of the best places in Africa to see sitatunga, a shy aquatic antelope with splayed hooves which spends its days in thick papyrus swamps. I've always had good sightings from Fibwe Hide, a viewing platform 15 metres up in a mahogany tree overlooking the Kapabi Swamps.

Another remarkable thing about Kasanka is that it hosts the largest known concentration of straw-coloured fruit bats. I timed my most recent visit for early December, when I saw over five million of them hanging like upended decorations in the Mushitu Forest. As soon as the sun had set, they would take to the sky, en masse, in search of food. I will never forget the sight of the sky darkening as the bats took off – it goes down as one of my greatest wildlife experiences ever.

Kasanka's main camp, Wasa Lodge, is situated close to Fibwe Hide and to the Mushitu Forest where the bats usually roost. There are nine chalets (four of which are newly built) and a thatched dining area and bar, with a balcony overlooking Lake Wasa. In winter, the sight of mist rising from the lake is spectacular.

At Luwombwa Lodge, there are guest cottages beside the slow-flowing Luwombwa River on the far side of the park. It's even quieter here and African finfoot, Pel's fishing owl and other specials make it a great birder's destination. There are canoes for anyone wishing to explore the river and the fishing is excellent. Like safari camps of old, water is heated over open fires and wholesome meals are cooked in wood-fired ovens.

Shoebill Island Camp in the Bangweulu Swamps offers a memorable excursion from Kasanka. The swamps, home to some 100 000 black lechwe, are frequently compared to Botswana's Okavango Delta on account of the incredible birdlife. Top of the tick-list for birders are the shoebills with their peculiar boot-shaped bills.

It's no easy task running a national park, three lodges, a fleet of vehicles, a community project and numerous game-scout operations so far from town, on a limited budget. The Kasanka Trust's contribution to conservation has not gone unnoticed, and the efforts of David Lloyd, who founded the project, were acknowledged by the Queen of England, who included him in her 2002 honours list.

Even more telling is the fact that the Zambian Wildlife Authority has extended the Kasanka Trust's management contract for a further 10 years on account of its impressive anti-poaching efforts.

PREVIOUS SPREAD Straw-coloured fruit bats, which concentrate in Kasanka's Mushitu Forest during December, take to the skies at sunset.

Home-baked bread and hearty meals are produced in the wood-fired ovens at Wasa Camp.

Shoebill storks are birders' biggest 'ticks' at Shoebill Camp, which is run by the Kasanka Trust on the shores of the Bangweulu Swamps.

THIS SPREAD Wasa Camp overlooks a lake where antelope such as puku, and sometimes elephant, can be seen drinking.

Fishing, birding and canoeing are all on offer from Luwombwa Lodge.

At sunrise, as mist rises off the wetlands, guests wait patiently in the Fibwe Hide for sitatunga to emerge from the reeds.

Sitatungas have thick, water-resistant coats, and splayed hooves that prevent them from sinking into the marshlands.

I've always had
good sightings
from Fibwe Hide,
a viewing platform
15 metres up in a
mahogany tree

details

When to go
Kasanka is open throughout the year. The best time to see bats
is in late November and December. Birding at Shoebill Island is
best just after the wet season, from April to July.

How to get there
There are charter flights between Kasanka and Lusaka and
Mfuwe international airports. From Lusaka it's a six-hour drive
to Kasanka. From Kasanka to Shoebill Island it's a 20-minute
flight or a six-hour drive.

Who to contact
Kasanka Trust. Tel. Kasanka (+873) 76 206 7957 (satellite
phone), e-mail *kas14@bushmail.net* or *park@kasanka.com*
or go to *www.kasanka.com*

travel advisory

Organising a safari

Either you can plan your own safari by contacting the lodges of your choice for further information, or you can employ the services of a specialist tour operator to coordinate your visit. In selecting your destinations and lodges, you'll need to specify your preferred style of safari. For example, do you prefer rustic bush camps to upmarket luxury lodges? Do you prefer walking to game drives? And do you like to spend time looking at birds and trees, or are you a first-time visitor who wants to see the Big Five? Give your operator as much information as you can to ensure that you end up with a suitable itinerary. An experienced operator will tailor-make one that works within both your budget and your scope of interests.

Africa Geographic Expeditions is the travel arm of Africa Geographic, and has good experience in tailor-making itineraries in Zambia. It also offer expeditions, led by experts, in Zambia and other African countries.

For more information phone (+27-21) 762 2180, fax (+27-21) 762 2246, e-mail *info@aspensage.com* or go to *www.africageographicexpeditions.com*

Cost of accommodation

Zambia isn't a cheap country for a safari because the seasons are short and it's expensive for the operators to run their camps. Most of the upmarket lodges charge upwards of US$400 a night, but some offer discounts at certain times of the year, so make enquiries.

When to go

The wet season is from December to April. During these months thunderstorms are common in the late afternoons. This is a spectacular time for flowering plants and birds, and the air is clear and fresh.

During the dry season from May to August the daytime temperatures are moderate, but the early mornings and evenings can be extremely cold. August to November is usually dry, becoming progressively warmer. This is a good time to see predator and elephant activity and the arrival of the first migrant bird species.

Getting around

South African Airways and British Airways fly to Lusaka from Johannesburg and London respectively. Nationwide flies direct from Johannesburg to Livingstone. Scheduled flights also operate between Livingstone, Lusaka, Lower Zambezi and South Luangwa. If you're visiting one of the more remote destinations, make your bookings for these first

as flights are less frequent. Note that the luggage restriction on light aircraft is strictly 12 kg, including hand luggage.

There is a regular and comfortable bus service between Livingstone and Lusaka.

Visas

Visas are required by most nationals, but the regulations change from time to time, so it's wise to check with your embassy or tour operator before you go. South African and UK tourists who enter Zambia as part of a tour organised by Zambian operators are usually exempt from visa requirements, if the operators make the necessary arrangements.

Money matters

US dollars, British pounds and South African rands are widely accepted. Most of the lodges also accept major credit cards. Remember to keep US$20 for departure tax when departing from Lusaka and Livingstone airports on international flights. For domestic flights the tax is US$5.

Medical matters

Zambia lies in a malaria area. It is therefore important to start a course of prophylaxis at least two weeks prior to your trip. You should take precautions against mosquitoes at all times of the year, especially in summer, by covering your body between dusk and dawn and applying mosquito repellent. Also spray inside your mosquito net before going to bed. The best way to avoid malaria is to not get bitten.

Clothing

On safari, it's best to wear cool, cotton, khaki or green clothing that will blend into the surroundings. You'll also need a hat and good walking shoes. Shorts are fine during the day, but long trousers and a long-sleeved shirt will give you protection from the sun, and are recommended for the evenings. In winter, you'll need warm clothes as it gets extremely cold on the escarpment.

Birding

More than 700 bird species have been recorded in Zambia. These can be identified in *Birds of Africa* (Struik Publishers, Cape Town) and in other field guides to southern African and East African birds.

Highlights on the birding calendar include the multi-species 'fishing parties' which converge on the shrinking Luangwa lagoons during the dry winter months. September to November are the best months to see nesting carmine bee-eaters in Luangwa. The biggest tick in Zambia is the shoebill stork, which is most easily seen in the Bangweulu Swamps after the summer rains. Summer is also the best time to visit Lochinvar with its large populations of waders, including pelicans and African skimmers.

Fishing

The best months for fishing on the Zambezi River are September and October, when the river is warm and low and game species such as tigerfish are most active.

Photography

Visibility is clearest and colours are brightest during the rainy season (December to April), but a more comfortable time is between April and June. It's very dusty in the dry season, so bring plenty of cleaning equipment. Also bring your own batteries, film and memory cards as they will be expensive and difficult to find.

Most of the lodges have 220/240-volt power with flat-pronged plugs as used in the UK, although some do use the plugs with three round prongs. To be on the safe side, bring an adaptor.

Don't forget

Binoculars are essential for game viewing. You'll also need sunglasses, sun block, lip balm and a torch. It's useful to have a pack of soothing travel sweets on dusty game drives.

AFRICA
Geographic

An Africa Geographic publication
published by Black Eagle Publishing
1st floor, Devonshire Court
20 Devonshire Road, Wynberg 7800
Cape Town, South Africa
www.africa-geographic.com

Reg. no. 1992/005883/07

First published 2005

Text & photographs © David Rogers
(with the exception of photographs individually credited)

Publisher Peter Borchert
Editor Mary Duncan
Art direction and design by Bryony Branch

Reproduction in Cape Town by Resolution Colour (Pty) Ltd
Printed & bound by Tien Wah Press (Pte) Ltd, Singapore

ISBN 0 620 33753 2

AFRICA GEOGRAPHIC EXPEDITIONS

Further information on all the establishments featured in *Zambia – Safari in Style* can be
found at the end of each entry. Your local travel agent or consultant should also be able to
provide help and advice. You are also most welcome to contact us at Africa Geographic
Expeditions, as we would be delighted to help you plan a visit to these properties or any other
destination in Africa. Africa Geographic Expeditions offers many superb itineraries designed for
the readers of *Africa Geographic* magazine. More about these can be found on our website.

Africa Geographic Expeditions
Devonshire Court
20 Devonshire Road
Wynberg 7700
Cape Town, South Africa
Tel. (+27-21) 762 2180
Fax (+27-21) 762 2246
E-mail *info@aspensage.com*
Website *www.africageographicexpeditions.com*